THE IDEA OF THINGS

THE IDEA OF THINGS

HOW THINGS REALLY ARE AS THEY SEEM

D W HOYLE

Orphir Press

Madison WI

Copyright 2021 Orphir Press

All rights reserved. No part of this document may be reproduced or transmitted in any form or by any means, electronic, mechanical, photocopying, recording, or otherwise, without prior written permission of the publisher.

OrphirPress@gmail.com   www.OrphirPress.com

dwhoyledw@gmail.com   https://orphirpress.com/DWHoyle/

ISBN: 978-1-7365509-0-8

Library of Congress Control Number: 2021931437

Contents

Table d'Hôte	vii
Acknowledgments	1
I. The Idea of Things	3
II. Things Happen	27
III. Thing-Esteem	53
IV. Things: A to Z	87
References	159

Table d'Hôte

I. The Idea of Things Lo! Hanging Fruit! *The Fruits of Ancient Wisdom* Yes, We Maybe Have No Bananas *Exactly 10,000?* Take the Amoeba. Please. *The Idea Machine*

II. Things Happen Misconfigured Fruit *Tops Down! Bottoms Up!* Primed for Primates *Things That Are Not Really Things* How The Leopard Gets Spotted *Another One Rides The Bus*

III. Thing-Esteem Things Have Feelings Too *Bewitched Benumbed & Bedazzled* Warehouse of Mirrors *The Not-Too-Small Matter of Cigars* For What It's Worth *Things Glorious Things* Halftime Report

IV. Things: A to Z Apple

Acetate Overlay Book Pages Advertising *Alphabet* Amoeba *Aplomb* Appendix *Armadillo* Bonnet *Book* Boot *Brass Rubbings* Breadbox *Bumper Saucers* Cap'n Crunch *Chicken* Chinese Box *Cigar* Cinema *Cookie* Clutter *Cookie-clutter* Coffee Collections Core Self *Dots, random* Dreams *Ducks, fake* Egrets *Food* Fumbyx *Fuzzy Logic* Games *Gander, proper* Gaslighting *Giant Stone Balls of Costa Rica* Hawthorns *Imagination* Jump *Kaleidoscope* Lamb *Liposuction* Magic *Mixer* Settings *Monkey* Movies *Museums* New Thought *Orange* Peashooter *People, other* Placebo *Plain, darkling* Priming *Quagmire* Quantum *Quotations* Reason *Regrets* Rock, pet *Self, the* Soap *Squirrel!* Tiger *Toast* Twain *Unused Letter* Verisimilitude *Warm Bath* Whitman's Sampler *Wine* Fez

Acknowledgments

The Idea of Things was conceived and written as a 'gateway drug' to the life-changing work of Antonio Damasio, Steven Pinker, David Eagleman, Chris Frith, Michael Shermer, Oliver Sacks, John Kihlstrom, Barbara Kreuzer and the many cited others whose sterling research is matched only by the range and depth of their insight and wisdom, with greatest thanks, appreciation, and admiration. Written in hope that readers of this droll and oft frivolous tome will be inspired to further explore the many rich dimensions of expression of these great thinkers and inspiring figures.

I. THE IDEA OF THINGS

Lo! Hanging Fruit! Open your eyes and you cannot fail to notice a world full of things. Every home has them. The great outdoors is rife with them. We use them in the kitchen, trip on them in the dark. Things are everywhere. When you close your eyes, they do not go away. Even if a burglar were to steal your things when you are in another room, or simply when you have your eyes closed, they are still somewhere. Things change, but sometimes our idea of them remains stubbornly the same. Think caterpillars. Think next door neighbors. Things can be incinerated, but we still have the idea of them that we always have had, even if in their current state they have become something more like ash.

When you go on vacation, the things you leave at home, they don't all go off on their own vacations too. They remain things in your home, but when you are in a lounge chair on the beach, and reminiscing about the paperweight you use at home, all you have is the idea of the thing, unless you brought the paperweight with you in your luggage, which most people don't, because there are plenty rocks on the beach that can do in a pinch. If you did not take your paperweight with you on vacation, and think about the paperweight while sunning yourself and drinking a piña colada, you can imagine how it looks, though you can't picture it in your mind fully in three dimensions; you only have fleeting mental images.

Everyone has a sense of the function of paperweights—what paperweights, in general, do. They know that just about anything can consistently and reliably function as a paperweight, except, perhaps, the cat. They can almost feel in the mind the force engaged by a paperweight holding down paper—mental imagery kicks into gear when you think about it—the dense, clumpy thing, the light fluttery potential of paper to fly away if the paperweight is not doing its job. You can virtually feel what it would be like to grasp the paperweight with your hand—how heavy it would be, whether it is colder than the air, the corners pressing into flesh. You know the color, any unusually angular features. You can have that idea of your paperweight with you your entire vacation, but hopefully you won't dwell on it too much, because vacations are all about getting away.

Then you get home. There is the paperweight. Uncannily similar to the idea of the paperweight from the lounge chair on the beach. Yes, the visual image is more static and consistent. Yes, physically touching it delivers a stronger sensory response than imagining holding it. But is it essentially different than the idea of the paperweight at the beach? Happily, physicists, neuroscientists and psychologists have spelunked cavernous lines of inquiry to directly address the essential questions. Thankfully, we no longer need to only rely upon philosophers, mystics and the clinically insane for answers.

In December, 2019 at an art gallery in Miami Beach, a constant milling crowd came to view a banana duct-taped to a wall. The banana and wall were attracting interest from art museums, though the objet d'art was ultimately sold to private bidders for $120,000. In the early afternoon, one of the exhibit visitors removed the banana from the wall and ate it. What soon made headlines was not, 'Man Eats Banana', it was that someone had eaten this particular banana, worth the equivalent of six Toyota Corollas. On a positive note, the artist who had created this unique and innovative work said that the eating of the banana was not a problem, since the banana needed to be periodically replaced by fresh bananas anyways. The gallery owner confirmed to the Miami Herald that the artwork was indeed not destroyed. What was eaten was not a $120,000 banana—the interloper had instead eaten the *idea* of a banana.

How is it, that at the same moment in time, a banana at Trader Joe's can cost 39 cents, and another one down the street can be worth three-hundred-thousand times as much? It is clear, that the idea of a banana can be worth more than whole bunches of actual bananas, and that the idea of 'banana' can maintain value even after any specific physical banana loses ~~a peel~~ appeal.

The Fruits of Ancient Wisdom   To calculate the extent to which all the things that completely surround us every waking moment—things seemingly absolutely everywhere—are an idea versus something concrete (or squishy, depending) it is worth looking at the whole of human history. Professor of Anthropology Donald Brown compiled a list of characteristics found in all human cultures, some of which are shared by other species, in *Human Universals*. Among these are: tools (things used to do things with); containers (things that hold other things); the lever (a thing used to manipulate other things); gift giving (a thing used to manipulate other people); imagery (picturing things in your head); and, hairstyles (picturing things on your head).

If these characteristics are found in all human cultures, including isolated tribes that heretofore shunned human contact, then it is fair to say that things are not a recent invention. Though the question remains: when in human history did people start having ideas about things? The oldest evidence of human activity on earth yet discovered are the Lomekwi Stone Tools of West Turkana, Kenya. These artifacts center on a 30-pound anvil used as a base for breaking larger chunks of rocks into tools. Despite the clear functionality behind their handiwork, we still have no way of knowing whether the West Turkanese thought of the fruits of their labor as 'tools', or simply as just more rocks, but useful.

It is one thing to use things to create other things that are useful, but things take a twist with the creation of things of little obvious practical value: art. The earliest evidence of art are the vessels and bones used for paint-making discovered in the Blombos Cave in Blomboschfontein Nature Reserve near Capetown, South Africa—a veritable painting studio with bright ochers from clay, red colorings from abalone shells, and charcoal for chiaroscuro. The ocher drawings on the walls are the first known cave paintings, although it is not clear whether the ancient artists had the idea of 'art', or knew they had invented the 'art gallery', as this was before written history when things were not given descriptive labels the way every item at the Victoria and Albert Museum and every animal at the zoo is today.

Not much can be known of the ideas our early ancestors had about things until people started using stones to carve patterns into stones. The earliest known of such carved hammerings is the Kish Tablet from Iraq, dated ~3500 B.C., with images of a foot and hand, along with pictographs that seem to represent early symbolic writing. The oldest known proper literature is the Kesh Temple Hymn chiseled into Sumerian stone tablets, dated ~2600 B.C., successfully translated in 1909, making reference to things of the time such as animals, houses, and landscapes, along with exaltation of people we will never know: "Will any other mother ever give birth to someone as great as its hero Acgi? Who has ever seen anyone as great as its lady Nintud?" the chiseled tablets ponder.

Whether this first literature qualifies as ancient wisdom is open to debate, particularly since ancient wisdom is a modern invention. These early texts appear more as itemization and celebration of favorite things, than philosophical rumination. From the *Egyptian Book of the Dead*, circa 1500 B.C.: "The days prior and the days after are redolent with the odor of pomegranates; the heart ripens like fruit and drops and breaks. Sweetmeat for the lips of gods. On such a day one glances toward the sky and the eye of Ra looks back. One finds loaves of bread on reed mats and the eye of Ra looks back. The air crackles. The sun beats on and on and on."

OK then. Things are discussed. Things are festooned with adjectives. But the awareness that we have ideas about things, and that things might not always be as they seem, does not come to the fore till religious texts attempted to take perspective on how we relate to the things that copiously surround us in earth's diurnal course. Prominent among these is found in Taoism, which arose circa 500 B.C. It is the idea of 'The Ten Thousand Things'. To wit:

> The Tao creates the one; The one creates the two; The two create the three; The three create the ten thousand things.

Not a perfect mathematical progression, and the Taoist 'Ten Thousand Things' actually has negative connotation, to the extent that the things relate to the corporeal nature of our earthly body lost amidst the world's endless parade of physical distractions, as anyone who has ever been to a shopping mall can confirm. The 'Ten Thousand Things' clutter the world and our minds, constituting the Legos under our bare feet in the dark on the path of our spiritual journey through material worldliness; but they are unavoidable, according to Taoism, as the things of this world are created by the Tao, by the formative tension between Yin and Yang, and we need to harmonize with these things, because we face considerable challenge if we pretend we can live without them. Sadly, in Taoist texts, there is no itemized listing of what the ten thousand things specifically are.

Problems with the epistemology of things—and the question

of whether or not they actually exist—reach escape velocity in the Diamond Sutra, discovered near a former way-station on the Silk Road. The Cave of the Thousand Buddhas is actually hundreds of caves and grottoes dug into a sandstone cliff. The Diamond Sutra was one of among approximately 40,000 prints and scrolls in the cave complex, most of which are still being digitized. The proper title of the Diamond Sutra is 'The Diamond That Cuts Through Illusion'—something as useful today, as it must have been back then:

> Thus shall ye think of all this fleeting world; A star at dawn, a bubble on a stream; A dash of lightning on a summer cloud, A flickering lamp, a bubble and a dream.

Although this passage makes mention of things that ostensibly exist, Buddhist scholar Kenneth J. Saunders explained that the Mādhyamaka school of Buddhism, "taught that the phenomenal world has no existence whatever; that it is unreal, as a flower in air, a hare with horns, or the child of a virgin carved in stone." To put the icing on the cake: ". . . all phenomena are unreal, or have only a relative reality; the life of man is either a dream or a total illusion." The Laṅkāvatāra Sūtra—another gem in the tiara of ancient wisdom—claimed that, "all things are mental creations: they exist only as a mirage, or a nightmare, and are produced by the mental impulse of a former time", in order to "produce a new illusion of being." According to Saunders, the view here is that the mind "not only colors and distorts all we see, it *creates* it."

Yes, We Maybe Have No Bananas   The fruits of ancient

wisdom seem to lead into a real pickle (not an actual brined-cucumber: 'real pickle' is a thing-free metaphor denoting a kind of metaphysical götterdämmerung). If the ancients were right that all is illusion, and that the mind creates all we see, then what difference does it make how much a banana is supposed to cost? This is where, in the modern age, the methods of inquiry and technological gadgetry of science can come in handy. The study of the brain, in the fields of biology and neuroscience, can offer the tools and perspectives necessary to validate scientifically—based upon physiological substrates—the factors and dimensions that condition how we perceive things (see, hear, touch, taste), formulate ideas about things (from mental images to wild ideas) and assign value to things (from big yawn to big bucks), in order to ascertain, in ways measurable & verifiable, whether or not fruits are just a fig of our imaginationment.

Take the fig. Light reflecting off the fig enters the eyeball. There the retina sends electrical signals through the optic chasm, along the optic tract, to a relay substation where multiple streams of optic radiation fibers feed the electrical impulses to the visual cortex—the part of the brain that has to make sense of all the electricity. None of the electrical impulses in this chain of communication resembles a fig. Multiple regions in the visual cortex have the responsibility of assembling all the coded elements into something figgy-looking: one region works on the shape of the fig, another the color, and another analyzes motion (in case it is a falling fig). Finally all the figgy features are farmed out to other brain regions and if you are lucky, and there hasn't been a routing mishap somewhere along the way like sometimes at the post office, there will be a visual image of something.

Something either greenish, purplish, or brownish (depending on whether it is a Kadota, Black Mission, or Brown Turkey fig) and either smooth or wrinkly (depending on whether it is fresh or dried), unless very bright light masks the color and surface detail, or it is so dark it could pass for coal. After the image is formed, other brain regions then need to define what it is. Those who only know wrinkly dried figs from the supermarket might assume that a fresh fig is an onion. Those who have never seen any kind of fig before might figure it to be a rock until they squeeze it.

All our senses work this way: they send electrical impulses along relays to sub-stations to regions that form representations that the mind can start to work with. Though only a narrow subset of what is out in the world gets sent up the chain of command in the first place. Bats hear so acutely and adeptly that they can find their way around pitch-black caves. Dogs smell and hear things we don't, and have a navigational sense to rival our hand-held GPS. Our amazing eyes actually capture less than .004% of the full electromagnetic spectrum. Our eyes are most sensitive to yellow-green (~550 nanometers), but useless for the ultraviolet and infrared that bookend the visual spectrum (however, those who do not have a lens in the eye, due to surgical removal or congenital condition, do in fact see ultraviolet light that is normally blocked by the lens as a whitish blue). As for microwaves, x-rays, radio waves and gamma rays, we only figured out they actually exist by inventing gadgets.

Neuroscientist Chris Frith in *Making Up the Mind: How the Brain Creates Our Mental World* sums up our situation: we do not have direct access to the physical things in the world around us at all. Our experience of things is an illusion, happening in the brain—a fantasy that, thankfully, can have high-fidelity similarity to what is actually out there outside our brains. What we take to be the physical world is actually a representation happening in our mental world. There is a momentary delay between what happens in the world and our internal representation of it, including the time it takes for the mind to figure out what it thinks it is perceiving, so that it can then decide whether to go ahead and step on it, or to pick it up and eat it. Psychologist Steven Pinker, in his vividly detailed explication of how the mind works entitled *How The Mind Works* references Plato, who compared us to prisoners held in a cave, facing a wall on which all that can be seen are shadows cast from a fire. The shapes and movements of the shadows are workable enough representations of people and things, but not the things themselves. Those shadows, those representations—as filtered through the conduit of our senses, and interpreted by the proclivities of our minds—are how we come to know the world around us.

In Plato's time, roughly 400 B.C., the prisoners would not have had the requisite gadgets to figure out what all the greyish two-dimensional shadows represented, nor to call or text any person attempting to make shadow animals to ask if the finger form was supposed to be a swan or a goose. If it was a coed prison cave, and baby prisoners were born, would the newborns as they become toddlers have any conception of what the shadows might represent? There is very good reason to suspect that they would. We are born with built-in blueprints for things: their shapes; how they behave in response to gravity; whether they bite or sting; if they are edible. If life were a play, which in many ways it is, we picked up the program when we entered the theater. If life were a ballgame, which in too many ways it is, we're filling out the pre-printed frames in the scorecard from day one. Admittedly, creatures like the bat, and the blue wildebeest (which can outrun a hyena within one day of birth) have a developmental jump on us cave-dwellers. They are 'precocial' species that know what to do, and can readily defend themselves from predators, and predict predators' behavior, right out of the gate. Humans are an 'altricial' species, which means that at birth there are still plenty of fig-identification skills, et. al., that still need to develop. In some European countries, humans take up to 28 years to be considered legally self-responsible.

At birth, human babies have difficulty telling two things apart; it takes till about three months for them to track moving objects with the eyes. What babies, even from birth, find most interesting is faces, and at the age of four months they are interpreting faces at close to a mature level. But other things are seen more in terms of orientation or dark/brightness at that age, as opposed to knowing the true brilliance of the thing that is a paperweight, let alone being able to recognize one. Those recognitions that baby sea turtles already master at the onset, do, sometimes at turtle-like speed, eventually kick into gear for humans, and the range of inborn knowledge is remarkable. Steven Pinker includes in the list of standard factory equipment: understandings of rocks & minerals, plants & animals, natural forces, and an essential logic about how things work in the world— including the feelings of others, and social dynamics. The world has order, and corresponds to the laws of physics. Infants are designed to interpret the world in those terms, beginning with their first actual encounters.

A fig might look like a rock, and if you have never seen a fig before you might not know what it is—but there is just something about it that makes it stand out in a field of rocks. Something, perhaps, tantalizing. Something ... fruity. Once old enough to toddle, toddlers are toddling the world recognizing and exploring precisely those subtle differences in the features of their environment that they were designed to know. Neuroscientist Chris Frith explains that we have hypotheses built into our brain not only about the colors of fruit, but also the particular color of ripe fruit. These hard-wired hypotheses have us develop ideas about fruit-like objects that we've never seen before. Subtle factors in shape, in differentiation in color, and the aroma of a lychee nut stick out in finger-licking contrast to a red rubber ball. Computers don't as readily reach the same delicious conclusions. For machines, the difference between figs and rocks isn't an automatic .It would take reams of code to program them with enough common sense to figure it out.

Exactly Ten Thousand? Trying to determine the exact number of things in the world is a sticky wicket ('sticky wicket' is a metaphor for being in a real pickle, but harkens back to the three wooden stumps topped by two crosspiece sticks in the game of cricket, where the wicket is an actual thing, but a 'sticky wicket' describes the predicament created when precipitation on the turf alters the inflection of the thrown cricket ball, making things chancy for the cricket batter.) The wicket itself is not sticky, it is the field-condition dynamics that are tricky, so a 'sticky wicket' is not an actual thing, but a circumstance.

If you check 'wicket' off the list, then there are 9,999 things left if one subscribes to Taoist inerrancy. In some ways, all living things can be conceived of as one entire living organism, with some very disparate parts, some of which swim in the sea, or fly in the air, or form giant fungal masses underground in forests—all of which interact with one another, albeit sometimes like Ford Mustangs and Chevrolet Impalas at a demolition derby. Anything we consider food is also a form of living energy within that larger being—one that before being eaten also previously sought out food, ingesting other parts of that single living being in order to increase its relative size and status within the one great big living whole.

If all living things are considered one quite considerable whole, that brings the total number down to 9,998. It is estimated that there are about 10^{49}-10^{50} atoms on earth (the number 10, with 49 zeroes behind it). Most people do not consider atoms things, unless they think about them too much. Instead, most people consider atoms to be building blocks that make up things. The idea of 'thing' is normally reserved for isolated and circumscribed objects or entities that people encounter. In 1975 over one million people, many of whom were unwrapping packages at birthday parties or white elephant sales only to stumble upon a 'Pet Rock'. A Pet Rock is indisputably a thing, but no child excitedly, with gleeful anticipation, ever ripped off wrapping paper to revel in the discovery of a 'Pet Atom'. Atoms cannot be collected, traded with your friends, hoarded, or arranged in semi-circles on the floor as a former world chess master is said to have done with women's shoes, and therefore do not easily fit the category of 'things'.

Other fudging that can be done with the precise number of things similarly involves aggregation vs. disaggregation. One can tally each blade of grass individually, or reduce the blades down to a single 'lawn'; though to reduce things further, all 'lawns' can be similarly subsumed under the greater category of 'grass', which brings the number down to 9,996 if you include the Pet Rock as a single entity, and not all 1.5 million Pet Rocks individually. Are bookends one thing or two? How many things is a box of Quaker Oats? Do you count each of the angels dancing on the head of a pin, or is it one single chorus of angels? Are 'a chorus of angels', 'a host of angels', and 'a pinhead of angels' three separate things, or are they virtually interchangeable?

The child with the Pet Atom, if asked how many presents he or she had just opened, if from a moderately well-off family, would probably say, "a gajillion", and if asked how many things there are in the world would probably also say, "a gajillion", and, in both cases, not to disrespect any religion or dogma, this is probably the most accurate response. The number of things in the world, are, however, vastly outnumbered by the number of ideas of things in the world. Thanks to the magic of adjectives. One single fig sitting on the table can be a lumpy fig, a wrinkly fig, a tantalizing fig, a sad-looking fig, an oddly charming fig, a forgettable fig, an inappropriately-situated fig, or a fig too small too big too hot too sweet or just altogether too figgy. This, before it becomes a flying fig.

Take the Amoeba. Please. With things thick as fleas, and ideas of things a dime a dozen, it can help to get down to basics by looking at the world from the perspective of a creature that has primal interaction with things, and no adjective-riddled ideas about things: the single-cellular, protoplasm-projecting organism known as the amoeba. An amoeba hasn't come to wonder whether bananas may be just a hallucination, and figs just a figment—it is spared that. Found in pond water, as well as in some less-fortunate intestines, and between two glass slides under microscopes in schools everywhere, amoebae negotiate their environment as shape-shifting blobs that can reach out and latch onto surfaces to pull themselves forward, or simply glide through water like Mark Spitz without the mustache.

If an amoeba, floating in an amorphous sea of liquid peppered by solids, like a peat bog, an under-chlorinated swimming pool, or the human brain, senses something in the environment it was born to avoid, it crawls or slithers away. It does not invent a pantheon of mythical beings to explain it. It doesn't perform elaborate rituals of jerking, scratching, rocking and tobacco-spitting like a baseball batter waiting for a pitch, to enhance the odds of success. Its nucleus is equipped with an array of automatic, dispositional responses to those noxious or toxic substances germane to pond life, sensed through chemical interaction. The membrane blocks certain substances and permits entrance for others, no goatee rubbing or Rodin-sculpture-like hunched pondering necessary. If an amoeba encounters something tasty, like a dead bacterium, it will expand its shape to engulf the morsel, and convert the energy from that former creature to energy for it.

Does the amoeba then hang a portrait of that dead bacterium in its personal gallery of culinary conquests? And post exhaustive details about the conflagration on Instagram? And modify categorizations of dead bacteria and records of their phylogenetic tree on file in the Library of Amoebic Studies? Well, yes, that is, in effect, what it does. The information gleaned from that encounter, which was made possible by the information gleaned from previous encounters across the lifespan of the species, becomes incorporated as essential knowledge for future encounters—much like the art galleries, Instagram, and Smithsonian Institutions of another particular species. But the media employed by amoebae are chemicals and electricity, not papyrus, oils, or jpgs.

The membrane and nucleus of the amoeba, like the museums and websites of Homo Sapiens, traffic in something very essential: information. English physicist Paul Davies can be credited with the recognition that it is not by studying how matter looks under microscopes, or what chemicals do in test tubes, or how photosynthesis photosynthesizes, that we can learn the secrets of life itself. That would be like dissecting your computer with a scalpel—slicing it apart circuit by circuit—to search for the secret of that great macaroni and cheese recipe your aunt downloaded off the internet. The essence of that great recipe, and of the workings of life, as Paul Davies describes, are not the different forms of media that convey information. The essence of life happening looks to be pure information itself. The chemistry, the circuitry, the canvas and the oils are the vehicles by which information gets embodied. And just as the amoeba has a nucleus, and the Smithsonian Institution has a Board of Regents, information can use ever more sophisticated superstructures, to make things even more informative.

The most advanced technology is now co-opted to use information in ways tiny creatures have been doing for eons. Take the self-driving car, or vice versa. These amoebae skill-level wannabes sense the pond streets around them and employ adaptive devices as necessary—based upon dispositional algorithms located in the 'autonomous vehicle driving control system', which is a kind of nucleus, or brain, or chipset. In addition to sveltely navigating the environment like the amoeba, and turning on lights when it's right like the glowworm, they also know just where to go like the monarch butterfly returning to the oyamel fir trees in Michoacán—thanks to a GPS system.

A decade or five ago, it took clunking, grating, screeching sounds, ominous odors, black smoke, or coming to a dead halt to let their human masters know that they needed feeding. But like dogs that yelp and cats that slink tight across calves, cars now have something even better: warning lights to show when they are hungry, and also if they are ill. While at the same time avoiding noxious pedestrians with no help from 'driver', who is now just along for the ride, like an oxpecker on a rhinoceros.

Self-driving cars can now 'see' better than any living creature. Not all living creatures have eyes, but most have photosensitive cells (these can't tell a rock from a banana, but help with things like the sleep cycle). Self-driving cars not only have eye-like cameras, but super-wide lenses that can see in all directions, like high-school teachers writing on the blackboard with mirrors in the corners of their horn-rimmed glasses. If it's foggy or dark they also have radar that bounces radio waves off surrounding objects, using the kind of 'echolocation' that birds, bats, dolphins, and whales employ. Also, like snakes who sense heat from prey in the dark, dogs who have infrared sensors in their noses, and mosquitoes with their uncanny knack for finding warm blood, thermal imaging cameras in self-driving cars can pick up longer-range radiation from anything that generates heat. But even the most sophisticated of living creatures do not have the 'lidar' that self-driving cars have. For precision in the most perilous of predicaments, like parking in puny places, the powerful system of pulsing lasers called 'lidar' creates 'point clouds' to plot positioning.

When all put together, self-driving cars draw from more information, across more dimensions, for circumnavigation than any living creature is designed for. The advantage a self-driving car has over animals is that it can perceive objects around it in every direction, using a variety of sensors, with superior accuracy. Sensory strengths are relative across animal species: * rats have phenomenal sense of smell, but poor, blurry vision; * bats can hear extremely high-pitched sounds, but cannot hear the bass booming from a self-driving car (they can hear the tweeter but not the woofer); * migratory birds have receptors for magnetic fields for navigation over long distances; * fish have lateral lines of pores on their skin to measure water flow and their relative speed—mapping their liquid surroundings. Philosopher and medical doctor John Locke said in 1693, "The only defense against the world, is a thorough knowledge of it," and a more thorough knowledge of things is made possible by senses that are finely developed across multiple dimensions.

Though recognizing that an object is in the way, is different than having ideas about things, and that is one area where self-driving cars lack the human touch. Self-driving cars also lack the ability to adaptively develop snow studs on their tires in blizzard conditions, or self-thicken their own oil in summer and then thin it again in winter, in the way that human hemoglobin levels change in adjustment to high altitude. They are wholly incapable of spontaneously generating any accessories not included in the original MSRP sticker price. They are completely indifferent if you kick their tires. They brake for small animals, but not out of compassion. They dodge and avoid things, but don't know what those things are. They don't know the critical differences between a mailbox and a panhandler. For such an advanced piece of machinery, the end-all and being-all of the brilliance of being biological isn't happening: the self-driving car has no feelings.

The Idea Machine   Plants, to their detriment or benefit, do not have a brain. This drastically limits their capacity to entertain ideas, and for ideas to entertain them. Instead, Mancuso & Fischer in *The Incredible Journey of Plants* point out that a plant is in its entirety a large, diffuse brain. Plants do learn from events and hold on to that knowledge—but that knowledge is everywhere in the plant, not in a chipset. Lop off half the plant, and the other half still has it. Lop off the part of a human being from the neck up, and that is all she wrote—even though the brain is only 2% of the human's body weight. Remove the whole big blooming cauliflower up top, the cerebrum, so that only the brain stem and hypothalamus remain, and the human will be in a 'vegetative state'. A person lacking cerebral functioning is sometimes referred to as being 'a vegetable', but Mancuso & Fischer report that vegetables are actually not themselves in a vegetative state. They are acutely aware of the world around them; super-sensitive; they sense precisely what chemicals are tickling their roots; they are sensitive to sounds like dripping water so they can seek it out; they have symbiotic relationships with micro- and macro-organisms; they are social beings who share with each other warnings about predators, and offer tips to attract pollinators.

Humans are also social beings, who warn others about predators, and offer tips for the trifecta in the ninth race at Hialeah. But humans are wired differently than plants. The wire that makes ideas possible is the neuron, a type of cell that plants do not have. The neuron is designed to communicate information over large distances in the body; the longest extends from the base of the spine to the foot. Neurons allow information from the body to travel to a central hub, where information can be merged and evaluated from a whole-organism perspective. From primitive nerve nets in jellyfish, to the 85-billion-fold call bundle primarily housed in the human skull, the principle is the same: a corresponding model is made of what is happening in the body, and in the body's interaction with the surrounding world. That model is used for coordination of responses—from planning how to fulfill basic drives, all the way to reflective problem-solving, and decision-making.

Professor of Psychology, Neuroscience, and Philosophy Antonio Damasio in his book that describes many parallels between microbiology and the entirety of human civilization, *The Strange Order of Things*, details the processes and rationales behind the mind making representations, so that the rest of us don't have to. The function of neuronal organization is to make a mapping—a condensed virtual mirrored reflection—of what is happening in the body. For humans, that reflective imaging of the rest of the body starts in the brain stem at the top of the spinal cord, beneath the big cauliflower of cortex. Monitoring the machinations of the body—along with some marionette-like string-pulling mastery over bodily actions—constitutes one atlas of mappings. But the brain also uses the same mirroring capacity to map the exterior world, by making mental representations of everything the body sees, touches, smells, hears, and tastes. It does so constantly, and voraciously. Every input to the brain sets patterns of neurons firing, making mental maps, and the patterns of firing change as fluidly and constantly as the body pulses and the world turns. The tingle on the hair on the arms, the blinking of the eye, the rumble in the gut, the darting of the chipmunk caught by the corner of the eye, the Lego under the foot—whatever is perceivable by the organism—if it's happening, it's all mirrored up there, relentlessly modeled by the patterned firing of the 86 billion neurons in the human brain.

Also mapped is the dance between what is out there in the world, and how the body and mind are constantly responding to it. How mood changes when the sky grows ominously dark in the middle of the day; the ease and quiet satisfaction of sitting out on the porch on a sultry evening; the salivating that happens at the sight of a lychee nut (once it has been established that it is a tasty fruit, and not a red rubber ball). The mind can reflect and think about these complexly shaded moments—and these reflections are themselves a new pattern of firings, a new mental map, a new idea. The mind makes maps of itself mapping its own maps. Like two mirrors directly across from one another, where reflections are reflections of the reflections, every thought thunk, about the last thought had, becomes a new mapping. Every idea about a thing, if thought about even briefly, becomes a new idea, as it puts a different twist, a different shading, a different time & experience stamp on whatever the thing originally was. The patterns of firing shift and blend and reconfigure themselves, every waking moment. This is what the brain is designed to do. It is a faithful, ever adaptive, uncanny reflection of the here and now (made possible by the processing power of that big cauliflower).

The amoeba, on the other hand, has only one cell to worry about. That is a lot less territory to map than the human body, which has ~30,000,000,000,000 cells. The amoeba does not have a single neuron, because a neuron is a specific type of cell, and the amoeba has only one cell: itself. It can't light up whole regions of cells in changing patterned configurations, like the 559 Christmas trees arranged in a maze in Manhattan's Herald Square on December, 2015 (setting a Guinness World Record), which would let the amoeba represent and then hold an image in its wild imagination of a noxious substance encountered in the pond. The amoeba does not have a wild imagination. Its memory isn't held in images, it is held in chemical changes. Antonio Damasio notes that nerve nets, bundles of neurons, like that of the 10 millimeter long squid-like freshwater organism the hydra, which has up to 100,000 cells, do use information from different parts of the organism to coordinate activity, and constitute a basic form of brain. But the hydra's nerve nets are not of the sophistication to allow a full mapping, a detailed representation, of any particular thing it encounters. Hydras can't hold a picture in the mind of the thing they are reacting to; they only know if it's attractive or repulsive. Hydras, with their nerve nets, still do not have a defined idea of what any thing is.

It is a matter of practical civic necessity, that the more cells there are, and the more different organs, appendages, circulatory systems, endocrine systems, (etc.) there are, the more an organism, unless it is a blessed plant, needs city hall to to coordinate things like the utilities, the food inspection, sanitation, and social programs. If a city has a sufficient range of municipal services, and they all operate smoothly, and no unit goes on strike, the town achieves homeostasis, same as do bodies and brains, livers and kidneys.

Making mental maps and models, filling mind with mental pictures, holding images in memory (tip of hat to Hiawatha)—it's the perfect setup for developing detailed knowing; for portraying, and elaborating, all manner of ideas about things.

II. THINGS HAPPEN

Misconfigured Fruit   In Oliver Sacks' classic detailing of neurological differences entitled *The Man Who Mistook His Wife for a Hat*, Dr. Sacks relates the story of the patient in question in the titulary circumstance looking for his hat, but instead reaching for his wife's head, and lifting it so as to put it on. The patient had a fully clear and workable idea of what a hat was. He regularly wore one. Also well-established was the idea of 'wife'. Dr. Sacks observed other irregularities: the patient confused parking meters for children's heads; he confused his foot for his shoe; when handed a rose he did not know what it was until he smelled rose; he could dress himself at home perfectly well while he was singing, but if interrupted, would be unable to know what to put on next; he sat at a table and ate cake but when interrupted, could no longer recognize the table as a table, or the cake as cake. The patient had lost the ability to recognize things by their thing-like image. His eyes were fine, but due to damage in cortical areas related to associations between visual processing & object recognition, he had the idea of a rose, but did not know what it was when he saw it. He could eat cake, but if presented with a cake on the table, did not know what kind of a thing the cake in front of him might be.

In *To See But Not To See: A Case Study Of Visual Agnosia* Humphreys & Riddoch describe how it is also possible to lose the ability to know what things are in relation to what they do. They describe a patient reaching for a screwdriver to cut paper instead of the available scissors, and when given an umbrella in the rain, holding it overhead without opening it. Another patient, when shown a hammer and nail, couldn't figure out how they related to one another, but when told the names of the things, suddenly knew what to do with them. The shapes of things were familiar to him, but he could not associate the shape of the thing with what function it performs.

Oliver Sacks was asked to see a patient who kept falling out of bed. As luck would have it, the patient would consistently wake up to find a big hairy leg in the bed right next to him, then would push the leg out of the bed in horror, and would then find himself on the floor. The patient certainly had the idea of 'leg', but as regards the frightening thing in the bed, the patient did not have the concept that the leg in the bed was *his* leg. Instead, it was like alien invasion. When Dr. Sacks asked him where, in all of creation, his own left leg might actually be, given his idea that the alien object was not his leg, the patient looked miffed, and said he didn't know.

The inverse is the phantom limb. Many who have had an arm or leg amputated feel sensations in that arm or leg, although it is no longer there. The sensations can range from feeling the limb is on fire, to feeling like circulation is cut off, to feeling like the limb is encased in a red balloon. The idea of the limb, and the idea of flexing muscles in the limb persist—as sensations are genuinely occurring in brain and spinal cord—even when the idea of the limb has become obsolete.

In an abundant expansion on phantom limb, neuroscientist Chris Frith reported the case of a woman, after a burst blood vessel, who felt she had three arms. She still knew—had the salient idea—that she only had two arms, but couldn't help but feel that her third arm was going to bump into things. When carrying bags in her very plainly observable two arms, she would still feel that a third arm was also carrying a bag. Chris Frith uses examples such as this to inform us that we do not actually have direct connection to the world; instead we have the benefit of sensory processing systems conveying signals, and our minds must make inferences based upon the information derived from those signals. In the best case scenario, those signals accurately reflect what is out there, and the inferential faculties of the brain work as designed.

Depending on circumstances, particularly in the case of brain damage, sometimes common-sense inferences don't fit what is actually out there—but the good news is that 'Man Bites Dog' type anomalies strike us as freaky. It means that we so much know what things are and how things should work that the examples from Sacks and Frith stick out like a missing thumb. And if something is amiss, in our base perceptions, someone is sure to let us know. If everyone were born color blind, we wouldn't have red and green traffic lights, as no-one would be able to tell the difference. As it is, for the 4.5% of people who are born colorblind, the idea that red and green are different isn't happening until someone informs them, and then attempts to explain the significance of the difference for the other 95.5%, particularly at traffic lights.

Tops Down! Bottoms Up! A burglar entering the home when you are on vacation might pick up the shiny object on the desk, thinking it valuable, and then papers start blowing away. The burglar might be thinking 'fence-worthy item', whereas you had thought 'paperweight'. Even with papers blowing away, the burglar might never realize it was a paperweight, unless this was a burglar who specialized in theft and fencing of paperweights. A paperweight thief might see everything: the Pet Rock, the Hummel figurines, and, yes, the cat, as paperweight. The paperweight thief is mentally primed for paperweights, the same way everything looks like a nail to a hammer.

It is when encountering something never seen before that hypothesis-testing needs to happen. Children first learning to read are put in high-demand situations requiring them to figure out what particular configurations of letters are supposed to signify. When coming across a cluster of letters they have not seen before there are two main tactics to try, and they are prodded to choose one over the other depending on what strategy is vogue in the field of education at the time: top-down or bottom-up. The bottom-up approach is called 'phonics'. The reader sounds out the cluster, letter by letter, in hopes that the mish-mash of sounds produced will remind them of a thing they know, and in hopes that the word is not the infamous 'ghoti', with 'gh' sound as in 'tough', 'o' sound as in 'women', and 'ti' sound as in 'hopeless confabulation'. Ergo: 'fish'.

Those born one or two years later down the road will enter school after upheaval in the curriculum & instruction echelons, and will instead be encouraged to use the top-down approach (also known as 'whole word' reading). Using this strategy, they will be alert to the context of the unfamiliar word, match the length and general structure of the word to their vocabulary base, and guess at what makes the most sense. Using the top-down approach, "Dick and Jane went down to the lake to catch a ghoti," is child's play.

When the mind encounters a thing, it employs both bottom-up and top-down approaches to figure out what the thing is. At some museums there are boxes for putting a hand into, to feel an unseen object, so as to guess what it is. At first, the experience might be one of hardness, or softness, or furriness. Hopefully not gooeyness. But until the 'bottom-up' sensations from the sense of touch align in ring-a-bell-like fashion with the 'top-down' knowledge of how different sorts of things feel, the predominant experience will be one of creepiness. Top-down knowledge can include the assumption that the thing in the box will not bite, since the museum would otherwise suffer lawsuits. Things that bite can be ruled out with a high degree of confidence. If there is insufficient bottom-up touchy information, and insufficient top-down idea-of-things information to come to a workable conclusion, the display will have an answer flap you can flip to find out what the thing in the box is. If, however, it turns out the object in the box is a fumbyx, those museum visitors with no prior knowledge of fumbii will still be left in the dark with a hand in the box, and will continue to experience creepiness.

If you see a small moving light outside in the night, but you can't make out what it is, it isn't creepy, it is eerie. The mind develops a hypothesis (which is a hazy, sketchy form of idea) about the thing. It could be an airplane miles away. It could be a firefly yards away. By applying preconceived top-down assumptions about airplanes and fireflies, hypotheses can be tested. As one point of comparison, airplanes go from point A to point B for some ostensibly meaningful purpose, whereas fireflies flit about willy-nilly for no intelligible reason. One tidbit of useful top-down knowledge about fireflies is that they do not bite (neither do airplanes, but this is of greater relative importance in respect to the insect hypothesis). Once all pertinent top-down knowledge checks related to both airplanes and fireflies have been exhausted, and neither fits the small moving light outside in the night, then the thing, by definition, is a an unidentified flying object. (UFO). The mind can then draw upon top-down ideas related to UFOs from a knowledge base honed by watching cable television in the wee hours, and the Weekly World News.

Similarly, walking through your child's bedroom at night in the dark, if acute pain suddenly is perceived emanating from one foot (bottom-up information), then top-down hypothesis-testing hastily clicks into place, like tumblers in a bank safe, to clarify the nature of the carnage. Chances are it is not a jellyfish bite, jellyfish not being native to bedrooms. In times of crisis, the mind seeks out answers to critical problems with particular speed and alacrity, and memory floods the mind with images of your child playing Legos that afternoon. Bottom-up meets top-down in a way that fits as nicely as Legos fit one another (not in the way that Legos fit feet). Pain being primal and self-preservational, the thinking happens instantly, leading quickly to generation of ideas, no matter how unkind.

Although bottom-up information is the useful raw data that changes from instant to instant, it is top-down information that guides our lives, because we have to have a pretty good idea of what things are before we encounter them, or else we are like infants staring out at a sea of amorphous blobs, including that annoying mobile. If we didn't already know what all those things in all those canisters the bathroom are we would spend half the morning reading labels every day. If you reach into the cookie jar, and you pull out a flat, brown semi-crumbly thing, you can assume it is a cookie. First of all, the outside of jar says, 'Cookie Jar.' Then, your experience tells you, that when you reach into the jar and pull out a flat, brown semi-crumbly thing, it has, consistently over time, been a cookie. If we didn't have routines like this—prior assumptions about most everything we encounter in life—then every day we would have to Google 'cookie jar' to learn afresh all about that ceramic cylinder, after which we would have to Google 'cookie' to learn about the different species of cookie, and what a disaster they are nutritionally. After sufficient research, one could then with confidence reach into the cookie jar and munch on one, and the next day, start the research all over again—though before going into the kitchen, it might be necessary to research what a kitchen is. Everything we do each day requires prior knowledge and expectations about things, that we don't have to consciously think about twice, or even ponder upon once.

Top-down processing will, however, lead astray if your innocent yet still creative child was making small cookie-shaped mud pies outside that day, allowing them to dry in the hot sun, then finding wild inspiration in their cookie-like nature. After entertaining the notion, the naturally clever idea might be to put the mud pies in the cookie jar. When you then, routinely, as part of an automatized behavioral sequence, reach into the cookie jar, and take a bite of the mud pie, at first, you might suspect nothing. The shape and texture is cookie-like. The crumbly feel in the mouth is cookie-like. The first chew or two are much like eating a cookie. The lag time for bottom-up information about the reality of hardened mud is nowhere near as potent and immediate as Lego pain, and due to the potency of preconceived expectation, and the sensual similarities, valuable time may elapse before the automatized top-down expectation of cookie is overwritten by bottom-up reality. Once the bottom-up sensory experience of mud pie taste and consistency conflicts sufficiently with the full top-down scenario of kitchens, cookie jars, and delightful earthy-sweetness—once a dissonance is recognized, and it is established that the top-down cookie script and eating routine may need to be altered—molars are already topped off with earth, and muddy rivulets are trickling menacingly toward the throat. All of this happening well before the onset of unkind ideas.

Primed for Primates The novice Zen practitioner is sometimes presented with ~~conundrii~~ conundrums for reflection, to gain insight on the nature of mind. One of these is, 'Don't think of a monkey.' What happens when someone seeking enlightenment, or anyone for that matter, is told not to think of a monkey, is that the spiritual aspirant, or anyone for that matter, will think of a monkey. Novice Zen practitioners have reported that when they try to comply, that the mind *fills* with monkeys, and that the harder they try not to think of a monkey, the more that show up.

The very mention of monkeys, to the constantly and voraciously mapping brain, not only creates a mapping of the words and actions of the person doing the asking, it also automatically generates a requisition to central storage for any related content to be instantly delivered up from the massive mental storehouse of memory for things. The monkey warehouse in memory may have detailed monkey knowledge—capuchin monkeys, howler monkeys, or the monkey wearing a fez with a tin cup on an organ grinder's leash in the Jardin des Tuileries—but when trying not to think of a monkey the mind will grab for the first generic monkey image it can find. (This will likely be a frisky monkey, up to mischief, because that is the monkey best fitting the mischievousness inherent in the impossible demand situation.)

If, on the other hand, the novice Zen practitioner is asked the opposite: to try to think of a monkey, and picture an entire, three-dimensional monkey in the mind—that won't work either. As Steven Pinker details in *How The Mind Works* mental images are at best 2 1/2 dimensional, never 3D, and things with angles and aspects defy being imaged whole A tail there, leaping feet here, a cheeky face with wide eyes and a sense of tentatively curious but insolent alarm there. All totally monkey-related, but no matter how hard the Zen practitioner tries to assemble foot, tail, face, and all the mischievous movements related to a monkey the picture is ultimately sketchy and ephemeral. The idea of any specific monkey does not get hauled whole in a single wheelbarrow from that monkey's cubicle in the monkey memory warehouse. Memories of things are assembled on the fly, in dappling monkey-related aspects, from disparate brain regions, each with a facet to contribute, but in the brain there is no whole monkey to be found, which is probably a good thing. The hippocampus (no, not the buildings & grounds of a university for hippopotami in the mind, but a brain structure that acts as a memory hub) generates the gist of a monkey, and activates regions in the neocortex that fill in sensory detail: sounds from auditory regions; shapes and pictures from visual regions; actions and movement from the basal ganglia. These shards and glimmers are shaped by the mind into a semi-robust mental image, one with just those minimal details necessary to fit the situation at hand.

If wanting to feed a specific animal at a petting zoo, or being attacked by that same species of animal in the wild, the mind will activate and assemble those elements of memory of the beast in question that fit the situation most vitally. 'Spreading activation' sends out a general call, like an ad in a Hollywood trade paper, whereupon the props, scenery, and actors that best fit the script, the dynamics of a situation, suddenly jump into the scene. When the order goes out to Central Casting to call up a monkey (or to *not* think of a monkey—same difference) aspects of monkey-related memory are needed to fill roles in the theater of the mind (ones that best fit the current plot of life).

Things That Are Not Really Things   Think of a thingamabob. There are two kinds of thingamabobs. One variety is the sort of thing that you might use regularly in the kitchen that you have well-established ideas about, but can't remember the name of. You know that the thingamabob is made of plastic, has a handle, and you need it right away because the eggs are in dire need of flipping. You know the shape and practical function, it is on the tip of your tongue, but the word 'spatula' does not come to mind, hence the exhortation, "Please hand me the thingamabob". This kind of thingamabob is indeed a real thing, it is just mislabeled. Although, to get technical, a thing that you have simply forgotten the name of is not a thingamabob, it is a watchamacallit. Also, if the thingamabob or watchmacallit is a practical device that serves a useful purpose, then it is properly termed a doohickey. If, however, the doohickey is mechanical in nature, then it should be referred to as a widget. Still, for any thing with one of these thingamajiggy names, the underlying object is still an objectively real thing. For each of them—the thingamabob, the watchamacallit, the doohickey, the widget—there is an entry in an encyclopedia or auto repair manual that tells the actual function and name of the underlying thing that the substituted word does not adequately represent. The substitute word is just a handy linguistic doodad.

The kind of thingamabob that is not a real thing, but is instead a disincarnate abstraction, is illustrated by the phrase, "It sure would be nice if there was some kind of thingamabob that could possibly plug the hole in this dyke." Failing the existence of such a thingamabob, a real thing, like a finger, will have to do. Nevertheless, there is still an essence of thing-ness implicit in the idea of a dyke-plugging thingamabob. If such a thing existed, it would be pliable enough to fit the hole, while also firm enough to resist considerable water pressure. Even the most non-existent thingamabob, has qualities and characteristics that can be conjured up by the mind—qualities and characteristics drawn from the vast mental warehouse of different aspects that viable things can have, with the potential of being given birth by the mother of invention.

Juliet speculated, regarding Romeo, "That which we call a rose, by any other name, would smell as sweet", but is a turkey baster by any other name (e.g., 'brother & sister blaster') still a turkey baster? For those who have not had the good fortune: a turkey baster is a fat plastic tube that tapers at one end. On the other end is a rubber squeeze bulb for suction and ejection of cooking liquids to keep roasting turkeys moist. They usurp kitchen drawers, and are unsightly, but do arouse fond remembrances of Turkey Days past, so are generally regarded with more warmth and appreciation than one might otherwise expect given their ungainly presence and uncomely feel the other 364 days of the year, and if the turkey baster had a more elegant name, something classy like 'spatula', it would have even more cachet. School-aged children, on the other hand, discover the turkey baster when on expedition in the kitchen, and may have no preconceived idea of 'turkey baster'—neither the name, nor the designed purpose—but on a hot day, they could easily devise use for it relative to the backyard wading pool. Their idea of the turkey baster would center on its delightfully comic appearance, amusing handling characteristics, and clear functionality in terms of wet mayhem, realized instantaneously, one might even say instinctually, in association with the inborn impulse to pester siblings. Not baste turkeys. An object with such magnificent potential for annoying siblings will awaken creativity lying dormant, activating such mental modules as use of tools, as well as understanding of the hydrodynamics involved in projection of fluids (practiced since spitting up on the high chair in infancy), along with deft timing for optimally-pestering delivery. These are things every child understands, even if they have no adult conception of 'turkey baster'. Still, despite the actual function as 'brother & sister blaster', the object in the drawer, to that child, will still be a 'thingamajig'.

The turkey baster, no matter what it is called, is a real thing, but consider the bus stop. A bus stop might evoke the image of a pole with a sign on it next to 30 feet of painted curb that demarcates where a bus will stop. You can determine if your bus will stop at the pole, and when it will stop there, using a bus schedule. A bus schedule is a piece of paper, or a web page, that lists when your bus will be stopping at that pole, barring the typical unforeseen circumstances. But the bus schedule is not the piece of paper, nor the web page. The bus schedule is an idea created by an operations department employee at a transit agency and shared with the general public and bus drivers alike. Even if they run out of bus schedules or the website is hacked, the idea endures that the bus will be at that pole at seven past, every hour.

If the bus company decides to have the bus stop somewhere else instead, but the pole remains at the stop, then even if the adjacent 30 feet of curb are still painted bus-stop color it is not a bus stop anymore, although it retains 100% of the physical characteristics of a bus stop. The pole and the painted curb were never really the bus stop—they have always essentially been the idea of a bus stop—just as the bus schedule is, basically, just an idea. The actual bus stop is, in fact, where the bus actually stops, and if the driver, unbeknownst to the bus company, becomes cognitively addled or rebellious, that could be anywhere. What was once your favorite bus stop, where you felt relief to arrive after a hike in the rain, where you felt a homecoming when disembarking the bus, where you shared that umbrella with your future life-partner—once the stop has been relocated, it is now nothing more than a bit of curb with a sad pole.

Is a haircut an actual thing? If you tell a friend that you like your friend's new haircut, the question is, what thing is it that you are referring to—is it how the head now presents itself with different lines and shapes adorning it? Is it the shape created by the cutting of the hair (be it bob, bun, bangs, bouffant, or pompadour)? Is it the freshness of seeing someone all-too-familiar looking different? The hairstyle is nothing you can really get a handle on (exceptions being ponytail and mullet)—it is an event that happened, resulting in a changed impression of the friend, or the head, or the hair. A slight gust of wind, and the hair changes again, sometimes terribly—it might look nothing like the haircut looked when it was freshly cut and first seen. If it were a real thing, you could swap haircuts with your friends, but no-one ever said, "I'm going bowling tonight—can I borrow your haircut?".

Consider the 'wedgie'. Can you see a wedgie? Well, if it quacks like a duck, it probably is a duck, but if it waddles like a duck, it could be a wedgie. But the waddling is not the wedgie, nor is it the undergarment that has been unceremoniously displaced that is the wedgie. It is more the act of giving a wedgie that defines a wedgie. The wedgie is not an actual thing, although it sounds much like one [well, it sounds like a widget]. You could never have a museum of wedgies, although it's surely been attempted.

Things that are not real things tend to a be an object or set of objects addled by a *disposition*. Antonio Damasio describes how the cortex is divided between areas designated to hold images (pictures, sounds, sensations) and areas designated to hold dispositions (automatic, pre-determined reactions). Dispositions are actions designed to happen in response to specific things and events: the tail of a dog that wags the moment the scent of a family member is noted; the cat that comes running at the sound of the electric can opener. Dispositions are mechanisms by which life gets managed—they are determinants of action, though they can also conscript images, to create pictures in the mind, of things that need doing—they can also use images to create a scene, so that the mind can test out different options and choices. Dispositions are the 'if . . . then' propositions guiding responses all the way from single-celled organisms up to the most conniving of creatures.

An amoeba's dispositions will have it either engulf something, or flee, depending, but in vastly complex organisms dispositional systems get gothic, and reach what might be their apex at the human cocktail party. Complex cocktail party behavioral algorithms require multivariately conditional recursive equations like: "There is food on the table but don't go straight over and scarf it down, instead wait until the party host invites everyone to partake; then don't be the first one there as that would look pushy, instead chat casually while approaching the table with dispatch, yet unobtrusively—then go for the healthy things that somehow manage to be actually tasty, but do not load up the plate so much as to look like a hog—and whatever you do, don't 'double-dip'". To achieve that level of dispositional elaboration across so many preprandial dimensions, homo sapiens have benefitted from an oversized cerebral cortex. (A big head.)

How The Leopard Gets Spotted Things can be nested within other things. A coin that fell from your pocket at your next-door neighbor's cocktail party is nested between the cushions of the sofa that are nested within the sofa which is nested in the living room nested within the residence of your next door neighbor. The sofa is a part of the living room, but the coin is not a part of the sofa—we have the idea that there is a sofa with a discrete thing called a coin in it.

Atoms are nested in molecules nested in cells nested in the appendix nested in the body of your next door neighbor, who swallows a coin, whereupon the appendix becomes inflamed, your next door neighbor is rushed to the hospital and the appendix is surgically removed, at which point it is passed to the scrub nurse, who takes it to the lab for pathological analysis, after which it is put into a biohazard waste container, wherein it then nests. The appendix was part of your next-door neighbor's body, but it is not now part of biohazard waste container—just like your neighbor is not part of the hospital. At least that's our idea of things.

A leopard has spots that are part of the leopard, but are also discrete things called spots. If you take a picture of the leopard with a 3-megapixel digital camera in landscape frame it produces an image consisting of rows of 2048 horizontal dots and columns of 1536 vertical dots making a total of three million colored dots, with different shadings and intensity of color. It is possible to make a disastrous photo editing error, vastly reducing the number of pixels, so that the image is 'pixelated'—the photo becomes a patchwork mosaic of just a few colored squares, like a Piet Mondrian painting, or a leopardy quilt with squares, not dots, for spots. It is also possible to zoom into a 3-megapixel image and try to determine the exact pixels that are part of the leopard and part of the background, and not be able to do so. The shadings so blend from background to leopard that deciding which colored pixel is leopard and which pixel is tree renders a craggy, jagged-edged leopard.

Still, our idea of what is leopard versus tree versus spots is very discrete, even if the leopard is hiding behind the tree. In statistics there is a rubric for deciding where one thing ends and the next thing begins. The statistical 'Markov blanket' isolates those specific nodes that are part of one whole integrated system (one 'thing') versus those nodes that are outside the 'blanket' (other things). Things outside the blanket are separate systems from the thing under the blanket. The things outside the blanket do not participate as an integral part of the functional whole within the blanket. They can only cause some kind of action or response from the thing that is within the blanket.

Our minds do a Markov blanketing of their own—they have an innate idea that things have boundaries, which is necessary (especially when there are leopards around) even when to the eye, there may be no clearly discernible boundary at all. Steven Pinker describes how the mind manages to make sense of a patchwork mosaic of shaded shapes it is presented with: determining where one thing starts and another begins; imposing upon the leopardy quilt an innate idea of boundaries; isolating useful or pertinent things, while relegating the less essential elements to the background. To do so the brain makes guesses, based upon inborn assumptions about how things work in the world, and what is in it. Our assumptions about what we will find when we turn the next corner come from life experience—from having turned corners before—but originated with inborn understanding of the nature of things. When there is insufficient information, like when there is strong glare, or it is dark, or the person has never turned that particular corner before, the brain uses assumptions to fill in the missing information—it assumes there will be more sidewalk—painting a mental image about what things are going to be like around the corner. Pinker calls the assemblies of assumptions and action-responses tailored to life demands 'mental modules'. Mental modules are strategic disposition bundles, designed for specific functioning in the world, that not only anticipate the shapes of things, but kick into gear to perform the many specific things that people daily do, ranging from identifying rocks, to avoiding snakes, to deciphering hierarchies of social status from subtle interpersonal cues.

Robots have far greater difficulty figuring out what is out there than your average toddler. Robots would need to be told that the spots on a leopard are not holes in the leopard, but part of the leopard. Since shadings overlap and perspective changes with movement, discerning one thing from another requires meticulous programming for robots, though it's automatic for us lucky non-robots. Humans immediately know from the flow of the fur of the leopard in motion that the leopard's got spots, and only later will ponder just how they 'just-so' happened to get there. Adding to inborn understanding of dimensions like angles, surfaces, color, and movement, are other cues—from prior knowledge, from context, from senses—such that if it moos, chances are it's a cow, not a large white leopard with black spots.

Antonio Damasio explains that any one sense, in isolation, can't adequately portray the world around us—it takes a team effort from multiple sensory sources to decipher a thing—and even that is still a partial rendering—but even partial renderings can be good enough for self-government work for an organism. James B. Gibson, in *The Ecological Approach to Visual Perception*, goes so far as to say that perception is designed only for seeing what is essential for the organism—we are not designed to know, and do not need to know, the full dimensions of what a thing is. It is the specific ecological niche that determines what that organism becomes equipped to sense. Gibson stresses that things cannot be perceived as what they fully and objectively are—instead, the structure of perception is determined by the needs of that species, and then further shaped by what it engages with in the world—such that even in the immersive wash of our sensory perception, we are still swimming in a sea of subjectivity.

What if you wake up one morning, and you can't see—but you don't realize it? This happens in a form of blindness, Anton syndrome, where stroke damage to the occipital lobe results in sudden blindness. Patients with the syndrome could start out on their daily routine without realizing they lack vision. The mind has warehoused the home they live in, in such detail, so vividly, that they go about their business as if nothing had ever happened, until they bump into something that is not where it's supposed to be. Dreams at night are similarly vivid, and detailed—an entire world presents itself—with bookshelves and Tiffany lamps—anything we have known in the world can be top-down conjured up for purposes of creating a convincing stage set with our eyes shut in the middle of the night, and those with Anton syndrome have that happen for them, even after they've woken up. As it happens, those with Anton syndrome eventually are frustrated by sufficient discrepancy that they wind up in a clinic, where they deny being blind—even as they can't navigate the hallways, trip over objects, or walk into walls.

Those who are blind from birth do not walk into walls. Those who come into the world without sight still innately understand that the things surrounding them have size, dimensions, and texture. They have a fully functional 'mental image' of the things they encounter—though it is not a visual image, and color will be missing. It will not be populated by the CGI visual cinematography that sighted people trot out from the warehouse, but it is a workable mental image for practical and thinking purposes. When walking around a corner, someone blind from birth will have more acute sensitivity to sound than most sighted people, and this will allow them to sense how open the space is. To the extent that things like cars and footsteps make sounds, that bounce off walls, they can make a mental map of that new street, and gauge the relative distance of things. The distance generated by sounds matches the number of footsteps away that thing is, just as bats can navigate a pitch-black cave using echolocation. The combination of sounds, vibrations, and things that are touchable create a multi-dimensional map in the mind functionally equivalent that of a sighted person—though lacking those elements of detail that vision would fill in. The idea of how the world is structured, and how things work, is something we are all born with, with our senses then filling in the paint-by-number details.

This ability to 'picture' things, without ever having seen a picture, is part of what Steven Pinker describes as the mind's basic language of thought: 'mentalese'. Say your stomach wants food. It doesn't have an interactive tablet with icons of different foodstuffs that it can use to select a pickle that transmits that image to the brain. It doesn't have a tummyphone to talk with nutrition central about its hunger needs and specific foodstuff preferences. Prior to sound, image, language, or teeth being applied to a pickle, there is the pickle impulse—a fleeting telegraphic transmission of the hint of the idea of pickle in the mind—in a word, 'gist'. Pickle gist—a communication that happens in the non-linguistic, not-necessarily-pictorial language of 'mentalese'. Even if blind from birth, there are building blocks of understanding inherent in mind, ready to be conceived of and share information in ways that don't necessarily involve pictures, and don't have to involve language, in order to make life in a complex world (but one that follows laws of physics) workable. Information is irrepressible, and constantly seeks out ways to inform.

Another One Rides The Bus French novelist Marcel Proust said, "The universe is real for us all, and dissimilar to each one of us." Even if we do not see eye-to-eye with others about the universe, the good news is that we can compare notes. We can simply ask someone approaching on the path how far it is yet to St. Ives, and how many are going. We can get a second opinion on whether a glass is half full or half empty. We can ask for an expert's perspective on whether a large random ink blot looks more like a hedgehog or The Battle of Hastings.

Each person's experience is a confluence of inborn structures, with individual differences assured by genetic variation, given content and substance by unique experiences, then warehoused in memory in splinteredly aspected ways, and recalled haphazardly depending on personal circumstances, but so many of us still manage to catch the very same bus. We will never know how much of what we experience when we are on the #24 to Pimlico matches others' experiences, but the fact is that 'bus' is a type of thing that, for most, is hard to miss. Busses are quite large, and are made of non-fragile materials. The number of fully grown adults who will not bail out of the way of a 15-ton projectile hurtling down the pike directly toward them is very small (and becoming smaller), and the same is true for squirrels and dogs, though deer do have a headlight problem, and the armadillo will leap three to four feet into the air when a vehicle approaches, which, in the case of a bus, isn't nearly enough. A sense of what to do when in the path of a speeding bus is fairly hard-wired for all humans, and it is certain that our hunter-gatherer ancestors on the savanna, with no idea of 'bus', would also have leapt out of the way of any interloping time-travelling speeding bus unless they took it for a spirit or deity predicted and promised by their hopefully now-extinct religion.

In *The Tell-Tale Brain*, neuroscientist V.S. Ramachandran tells that as we navigate our way through what we assume is the world, that, in a sense, we are hallucinating, constantly. However: perceptions of objectively real things are indeed part of the mix. Many of the things that appear in the constant flow of the mind's eye are perceived with sufficient accuracy (e.g., speeding bus) to provide an 'anchor' of reality in the world around us. These real-thing anchors allow us choose the hallucination that is most appropriate to the practical ramifications of, say, standing in the middle of the road. We can separate the wheat from the chaff, the speeding bus from random daydreams of pink elephants, in meaningful ways that keep us from getting hit by the thing that is bus. Dr. Ramachandran describes perception as the ongoing process of choosing the hallucination that is most fitting to our encounters with the outside world. He notes that in situations such as dreaming, or being in a sensory deprivation tank, there are no such anchors. Dreams are free to go places without the anchored corrections that going around town during the day makes necessary for survival. Pink elephants can cavort happily in dreams, but not so much on city streets.

Chris Frith also explains that we model the world through a kind of fantasy that hopefully is a good match for what is actually out there—and beyond that, if the senses don't provide enough input to portray a bus, our brains will color in the picture with its own (top-down) projections using the best available clues. Our minds fill in gaps in perception and experience so that the world looks like a whole, continuous, world, similar to the way it smooths over the blind spot in the eye created by the optic disk, where there are no photoreceptors. What we see, and experience, of the world seems seamless, thanks to a brain that will not permit gaps on the mental movie screen showing today, at a theater in you.

To perform gap-filling the brain must have top-down assumptions about what it out there. In the case of the blind spot in the eye, it is a smudgy matter of filling in the spot with the colorations surrounding the spot. In the case of hearing, if there is a sudden loud noise, people will fill in a missing word, perceived as an actual sound, even if the sound of the word was completely blocked by the loud noise. The process can also go overboard: people who lose their vison and develop Charles Bonnet syndrome often see people, landscapes, and myriad things—it is as if the stage of action that is the mind insists upon filling in the gap that is loss of vision, with random warehouse scenery from the memory backlot.

Top-down prediction is powerful. Frith says that it is this prediction—expectations of what we will find in the world—that actually initiate the chain of perceiving, and that the input we receive from the senses then adjusts and conditions the expectation model. Any discrepancies between what is expected and what shows up when boarding any particular bus are registered, and mental models are then changed, leading to improvements in quality and accuracy. The hulking form approaching on the road in the distance: is it the #W15 to Hackney Town Hall, is it the #308 to Clapton Pond, or is it a Mr. Whippy? Sometimes we assume it's one but it turns out to be the other, once we can clearly make out the sign, or spot the massive plastic ice cream cone on the roof. But when in doubt, and the anticipation becomes unbearable, we can always ask another rider waiting at the bus stop who has better vision, or ask a child, as children have particular alacrity for spotting ice cream trucks. The gift of language has made it possible to quickly and broadly communicate information—to better identify, hone, and come to agreement on the nature of things, as well as to share knowledge about things that are situation specific. It is one thing to understand a bus as a 15-ton projectile, and quite another to know what route it takes, whether the driver can make change, and whether live chickens are permitted onboard. Those kind of bus understandings we are not born with—they derive from culture, and are shared by others, on a need-to-know basis. Someone living in the culture of London will also want to know that a bus will halt for anyone standing near the Lolsworth Close, Spitalfields stop, but that to board a bus at Shaftesbury Estate, Battersea, they will need to wave an arm or the bus will pass on by. We do not have species-wide instincts specific to the Hail & Ride system in London, and the list of stops affected are not embedded in our genetic code.

Sharing knowledge allows those with optimal insights to make things easier for others. At the bus stop, one punter might be nearsighted, another might be color blind, and another might have a pair of binoculars. Each individual has a unique set of sensory skills (which can be enhanced with technology, like binoculars or a bus app) and each has their personal range of background knowledge (like knowing that the #W15 is single deck and the #308 a double-decker). This will allow anticipating riders to come to a general consensus well before the arrival of the bus (unless one of them is prone to confabulation or hallucination). If all else fails, wave the arm just in case, and when the vehicle stops ask the driver if it is the right bus, or if they have a Frobisher & Gleason raspberry flavored ice lolly.

Antonio Damasio states simply that if we want to learn more about our world—but also about the subjective nature of each individual's perceptions and perspectives on the world—we can ask them, and has employed this as a vital method in medical, psychological, and existential inquiry. Although we each experience things differently, there is generally enough similarity in our human constitution as we experience the world, that by comparing notes, we can come to an understanding, if not wholehearted consensus. We may each individually (or as a species) have constrictions in perception, and we each might interpret what we experience differently, but by sharing perspectives with others it is possible to refine our understandings, and come to meaningful agreement, with increasingly high fidelity, including if it is the bus to Clapton Pond.

III. THING-ESTEEM

Things Have Feelings Too Putting a quarter in a gumball machine: the satisfying click of the snug fit—the shiny disk of monetary value with pleasantly reassuring George Washington wearing half a smile, ready to go for a spin. Looking up at the big bulb of glass holding the gumballs: a wonderland. Big time anticipation for a child of any persuasion, needing no persuasion. The yellow gumball looks like a burst of promise. The purple gumball: please not purple; anything but purple. The red gumball on the other hand: ripe dynamism. Turning the crank—each sharp click a stab of excitement, until release with the sound of hollow rattling of gumball tunneling down the metal pipe. The fun little metal hinged flap wags open with a burst of happiness, before taste sensation happens. Each thing—from the gleaming value in the coinage to the clicking mechanics to the color of each individual gumball—evokes a response, while shrouded within that general warm bath of joy that is being allowed by parents to have candy, after all that excruciating begging.

It doesn't stop with gumball machines. Too often it starts with the sound of the alarm in the morning, which also evokes a feeling (one that uncannily matches the name of the device). The softness of the bedding: cozy sensual bliss, a half-dreamy fondness and attachment, followed by the feeling of sober regret that is getting out of bed. Having the foot land on the one Lego missed while picking up the night before, evokes a different feeling. All the day through is a progressive navigation through a swirling symphony of feeling, one sensation after another, pursuant to the last, blended with the next—mood and tone shift with exposure to each and every thing encountered: things alluring, disconcerting, or comfy like a warm sweater.

Each individual thing evokes qualitative impressions, but the body too chimes in with feeling across a range of dimensions. You might be paying no attention to your toes, and how they are feel, till you think about it. Then they feel like something. There is generally no reason to think about them—unless they step on something untoward, in which case there is no *not* feeling them. You can't feel what your kidneys are doing, since the central nervous system, in its adaptive wisdom, spares us having to feel what our internal organs are constantly up to. It just isn't necessary—and it would be a mood madhouse. If something goes wrong with an organ, another part of the anatomy, the tum perhaps, or a lightheaded-feeling head, is likely to eventually suggest that something is out of sorts, and lead to an action, like googling symptoms or taking a pill.

Antonio Damasio titled his book *The Feeling of What Happens* deceptively simply. It speaks of the role that feelings have in not only letting us know 'how we feel' but feelings also generate our very sense of being a thing, of being alive. The feelings the body generates (initially to let us know if things are well, or if there is damage, or danger), also spurred by internal motivations and drives, interact with what engages us in the world to create a constantly shifting qualitative state. From the moment of the alarm till when we nightly check out, feelings are an all-day affair from consternation to bliss, excitation to ennui. Even boredom is a feeling. Neuroscientist Christof Koch in titling his book *The Feeling of Life Itself* also confirms, in case people haven't noticed, that being conscious *feels* like something. There is always an atmosphere; it can be thick like pea soup or thin like prisoner's gruel, but being alive is very much palpable; it has flow over time, held together as the idea of 'consciousness' by trains of thought.

Like jellyfish and pond snails, humans have nervous systems that provide non-stop information to a central command structure about the state of the Markov-blanketed whole thing that is the body. In central command, that information is felt, as feelings. When the senses send information to the mind, which then determines that a green oblong object is a pickle, the body then responds with feelings about the pickle. If the body has been sending hunger signals for some time now, feelings may have a bright, excitatory 'eureka' quality to them. But if it turns out to be a soggy, squishy pickle, the mental module of 'disgust' may come into play. Central command must then use its cost-benefit dispositional algorithms to decide whether to eat the soggy, squishy pickle anyways, with the ultimate goal being to enhance well-being, and reduce displeasure or discomfort. That is the job of the brain all day long: 'Ac-Cent-Tchu-Ate The Positive' while avoiding misery. Feelings are the intricate arbiter of that process, and the sum total of feelings turns out to be the sense of being alive.

Each thing held in awareness has a feeling quality, and the moment sleep has ended we find ourselves surrounded by things. They can't be avoided. We need a floor under our feet to stand on, a vessel to drink from, a toothbrush—the list is endless, and things are all-pervasive. Ten thousand might be a conservative estimate for the average middle-class home, and each thing has a qualitative sense to it too. Damasio tells that every thing we perceive in the world around us is run through an emotional qualifier before it reaches our conscious awareness—the very process of sense perception has a feeling-filter that tinges the things we encounter with a valence, be it positive, negative, or tentative indifference. But there is no perfectly neutral gumball if your attention falls upon it. Attention requires evaluation of a thing, and it generates a response. It could be an attractive gumball, or an off-putting gumball; a gumball you want to avoid stepping on, or a rolling gumball that needs to be caught before it escapes under the sofa. The subtle inflections of feeling-responses a gumball may arouse do range at times to the almost relatively neutral (some people aren't really all that interested in gumballs), but even that neutrality is a weighted balance. Feelings are always there, though we may attend to them minimally, or attend to them with focused attention—and some things just do not require a lot of attention. When we wake in the morning, the optimal surroundings are one of mostly minimally-attended-to comfy-sweater-semi-neutrality, peppered by more vivid joys.

Turn the corner and a broad, open street with gleaming lights from upper floor windows gives a sense of space and expansion, options and promise; versus turning the corner into a dark narrow alley. Walk another 20 yards and approach the Department of Motor Vehicles, and feel the trepidation, the little shiver. The crumbly concrete steps and chipped handrail convey old, ill-kept, ill-funded institutionality. Enter and the hoary lighting, the stark yellowed hallway walls, give a feel of a place where nobody is happy, including many who work there. Enter the license renewal room and be assaulted by jarring lighting, too-many other licensees sitting slouched and sullen in uncomfortable metal & plastic chairs, and take a number. None of these things are good omens. None. Everybody there is trying to diminish their interaction with the place, and the feelings the place evokes. Some have even taken mind-altering substances just to try to minimize the impact of the feelings that tend to ensue from being in a dullish, sometimes threatening place. No-one is able to flee, as any sensible amoeba would do, when confronted with similar circumstances. But the human being knows that the ramifications of being pulled over while driving without a valid license, are even more to be avoided than sitting around for forty-five morose minutes at the DMV.

Whether it's alarm clocks, Legos, toothbrushes, leopards, gumballs or the hard-plastic metal-legged chairs at the Department of Motor Vehicles, all things wind up evoking some kind of feeling, and once attention is drawn to a thing feelings accompany the perception, and once thinking happens about the thing being perceived with its accompanying feelings, ideas are born, that in turn alter the perception of the thing—all of which is then encoded more or less in memory: feeling-tinged memory not just for whole objects, but also diverse aspects;

different colors, sounds, shapes, textures can all evoke feelings independently, and can carry over to lend tone to other contexts in turn. Years later the gumball machine scene may be wholly forgotten, but the grown adult at the paint store, when looking at paint sample chip cards, might insist on the gumball-yellow for painting the garage, with no real idea why.

Warehouse of Mirrors The Hall of Mirrors: the resplendent jewel of the Palace of Versailles, marble walls, thirty Charles le Brun paintings on the ceiling, forty-three crystal chandeliers, and 357 mirrors positioned to reflect the light from the gardens and make the long passage, only 34 feet wide, seem endlessly expansive. Every glance in the hall of mirrors spans multiple reflections of things also in direct view, though each perspective is different due to the different angles of mirror, and slight mirror imperfections. The brain: a hall of mirrors, where every image that comes to mind lights up chains of mirroring associations, each with feelings attached, yielding a new composite image that the mind then models, and then goes on to make mirrored models of the new models of the models it just made. If you have an idea in mind, you can then have an idea about that idea, which permanently alters the original idea, that in turn can be seen from different perspectives altering the changed perspective, making the human imagination like souks in the medina, with endless passageways turning in upon themselves, all arrayed with curiosities, shifting atmosphere: marvels to marvel over.

It pays then, to go to the store and buy something nice for the home, to pleasant up the passageways and richen up the rooms. Not something in a Department of Motor Vehicles motif, but something that will have pleasant associations. The things that people arrange about an abode, evoking feelings as they do, and triggering associations that populate the mind with ideas and mood—it's worthwhile to pick up things that make life feel charmed, not numbing, pleasing, not frightening, as neutral is very hard, if not impossible to find.

Take the Hummel figurine. Please. Originally designed by a nun named Hummel, the small porcelain sculptures of chubby children holding umbrellas, geese, and other things of the cutest possible variety took off after their introduction at the Leipzig Trade Fair in 1935, exacerbated by American soldiers buying them as souvenirs, leading to manufacture of over 50,000 figurines each year into the 2010s before the hysteria died down. The rosy cheeks bring a sense of wholesomeness and well-being; the fully dilated eyes suggest full engagement with life or eating the wrong wild mushroom, juxtaposed by the coy innocence of a slightly cocked head; the dirndls and the lederhosen bring a sense of tradition, of a time gone by when everyday clothing reflected sartorial expression within a frame of reassuring cultural consistency; the fat little legs with feet stuck together speak of humility, and give assurance that they are not going to run away and leave you too quickly; the goose suggests the abundance of having plenty to eat; the over-sized umbrella represents an aura of shelter and protection; the accordion the spirit of conviviality and the old-fashioned meaning of gaiety. This is the sort of thing people want to have around the house, because every glance brings wheelbarrows of associations out from their respective feeling-besotten warehouses. A whole collection of Hummel figurines—one with a beer stein, another playing the violin, another with bunnies: ideas of things fill the home, and the imagination.

Surroundings, as a whole, or as a sum of its parts, can be enhancing (rocking chair; front porch; near sunset; with tasty beverage) or enervating—though it could be that a DMV is not so bad, like the DMV in Mount Pleasant, in South Carolina, which in June 2020 had all of ten 5-star and eight 4-star ratings on Yelp; glowing reviews, though mostly lauding the getting in and out quickly. The front porch as evening draws in, when the day's toil is past, with dominion over the yard, expansive views to all the activity in the environs, warm colors in the sky with tinges of red promising a bright morrow, birds-a-tweeting to tell all that all is well; a scene of calm, life-mastery, promise, ease, and well-earned satisfaction (particularly the beverage) that still beats even the most pleasant Mount Pleasant DMV.

In the home, décor can be minimalistic. Near spartan simplicity, highlighting essential elements of daily being, allowing space for the imagination to travel in fine straight lines, uncomplicated by Hummely encumbrances. Or a home can be a veritable Grand Central Station of bric-a-brac, knick-knacks, bagatelle, gimcracks, and things to be organized at a theoretical later date. Either way, the clean lines or myriad stuff inevitably act to shape a mind that abhors a vacuum, and will never experience one, except perhaps in delta-wave deep sleep or coma. For most, the things in the home do not come alive in the same way that the broom, clock, candlestick, teapots and teacups in Disney's *Beauty and the Beast* dance around with inimitable personality and attitude, but individuals do have a greater or lesser propensity to see human qualities in inanimate objects, and may give their boat or their car, or their vacuum cleaner a name to match. But one thing is guaranteed: a stranger entering the home will never have identical feelings that match those of the resident. In fact, it is possible to enter the home of another and find the very treasures that give meaning and succor to the inhabitant near insufferable. Though it is possible to fall in love with the resident, and then have the same sea of objects that previously proved insufferable glow instead with warmth and beauty. Feelings about things are malleable.

There are places intentionally designed to be near insufferable, like prisons. Photographer Sina Niemeyer toured prison cells in Lower Saxony, Germany where inmates were permitted to decorate their cells as they pleased. Inmates were generally proud of their items of choice, except for the one inmate who left his cell completely bare as a form of self-punishment. Most common, besides the television, were family pictures, racy pin-ups, and flags of nations or soccer teams. Inmates filled their otherwise spartan sphere with pictures and symbols having strong personal associations, with bits of art and stylish design also in the mix. One particularly well-embellished cell, belonging to an inmate sentenced for armed robbery, drug-dealing, and human trafficking, included a wall adorned with hand-made beadwork, playing cards, racy pin-up, a colorful calendar, a picture of a beach scene with palm tree, and a draped fabric image of a tall-legged bird in a flowery swamp. Though what struck the photographer markedly was how common it was for inmates to place curtains over the windows, kept drawn even on pleasant days. The inmates did not want to see the bars on their windows. In creating a sphere of personal meaning, little joys, and general comfy-sweaterhood, the bars were an ill pill. The opposite of front porch.

For the inmates in Lower Saxony, interior decorating was their only real freedom in confinement. What they were ultimately decorating was their mindscape—shaping a textured weave of feelings while in their enforced state of suspended animation. There are prisons that have allowed inmates only toiletries and a Bible; anything else displayed would be ripped out. As the one inmate in Lower Saxony who denied himself all things knew, the inability to shape one's own world with rich resonances is punishment, not habilitation.

Bewitched Benumbed & Bedazzled It gets worse. It gets worse, particularly, in the company of bugs, rats, and slithery things. The most popular unpopular things, according to psychological professionals, are snakes and spiders. People are born with high-potency dispositions that kick into gear in the presence of snakes and spiders, assuring their unpopularity. People who are afraid of spiders can be considered smart. However, about 5% of the human population, according to researchers, could be considered *super* smart, as they qualify as having 'arachnophobia', which is defined as 'undue' anxiety about spiders, which brings into question the definition of 'undue'. Luckily, since time immemorial, psychologists have been employing ~~tricks~~ therapies to help people halfway tolerate normally intolerable things, and have success with spiders.

To shape undue fear of spiders into a more due one, one approach is 'systematic desensitization', which involves exposing arachnophobes to spiders gradually, in a safe and soothing situation. At first the spider might arouse paralyzing fear, but after the spider is withdrawn, calm is restored, soothing renewed, and when the spider comes back in successive exposures, the fear becomes successively diminished. The novel experience of a spider, in this different feeling context, changes the automatic reaction to spiders in ways that carry over to other life situations.

There are some arachnophobes (geniuses?) who cannot even tolerate the first exposure to a spider, even in a calm, supportive situation. For them, Granado, Ranvaud & Peláez devised a systematic desensitization protocol that exposed them to things that could in some ways remind them of spiders. Just as simple exposure to a single color or scent or angle can spur the mind to connect the dots and come up with the idea of an entire thing, they exposed the brilliant arachnophobes to images that in abstract ways would evoke a splintered sense of spider: Gothic cathedral spires; a spindly-legged tripod; a swing carousel at the fair with chairs on chains spinning (as if they were eerily crawling) in the air; and the Atomium in Brussels, which is a 300-foot tall steel model of an atom that actually looks a bit like a cross between a spider and a spider web. Although each image evoked spiders in each subject to a different degree, which is to be expected as we each encode and associate things differently, participants experienced significant improvement.

To mitigate discomfort, or the gloom that can ensue in suboptimal situations, some people still prefer narcotics. Certain chemicals obviate feelings almost entirely—feelings that range from subtle to overwhelming—from the wee bit of satisfaction when a match finally catches flame after multiple scrapes on the worn striking surface of a matchbox, to mortal terror related to deadly insects. Isoflurane, desflurane, and sevoflurane are some of the most effective feeling inhibitors, as they induce general anesthesia, leading to immobility, loss of consciousness, and absence of feeling whatsoever. Those with only mild undue feelings generally consider this too extreme. Opiate addiction also reduces the potency of everyday feelings—things like the mellifluousness dappling of raindrops in the garden, the frustration of an irretrievably buried ace in online Solitaire, the little gasp of joy when the orchid on the windowsill blooms, spam phone calls, the satisfaction of being praised at work, the flush of surprise and elation when catching the wedding bouquet—*all* of that is paved over with a warm flatness like new asphalt on the highway—all replaced by one big opiate feeling. The downside with numbing one's responses to things that are unpleasant, is that it also numbs responses to everything else. Whenever possible, it is better, when a thing displeases you, to change your idea of the thing. That's why tricky psychologists also employ 'cognitive reframing'. Reframing changes what associations are hauled out of which mental warehouses—the 'web' of associations about things like spiders gets shifted. The arachnophobe might study spiders—learning about their behavior and habitats, their talents and passions, in a more sympathetic light. Or practice thinking of them as more cute & fuzzy than prickly. Or imagine them in their underwear—whatever it takes to shunt the tracks of spider ideation along more positive pathways, so that ideas come to mind that monkey up the fear response.

This works for most any thing, not just for the most creepy, deadly, creatures on the planet. A glass that is half full, can be reframed as a glass half not full. The family heirloom vase that junior knocked over and broke, can be seen as having character and craggy charm as a paperclip receptacle. The obviously already considerably re-gifted birthday sweater: at first it evokes disappointment, but with a little ideational tweaking it can become an iconic source of mirth every time it is passed over in the closet, or when it is re-gifted anew. In the case of a banana duct-taped to the wall, instead of thinking, "There is a banana duct-taped to the wall—big deal," a person could shape-shift the response into, "There is an elegantly positioned, lustrously semi-ripe, brilliantly juxtaposed, artistically intriguing, cheekily irreverent banana cleverly duct-taped to the wall, worth $120,000. Looks delicious."

Once the new idea is entertained, the old idea of the thing will never be the same, or as American transcendentalist Ralph Waldo Emerson said, "The mind, once stretched by a new idea, never returns to its original dimensions." Altering the idea of a thing, by forging new associations, can radically change the predominant feeling that the thing evokes. This tactic found great success in Pele's Curse, made popular at Hawai'i Volcanoes National Park. Park rangers or bus drivers at the park, it is speculated, grew frustrated with tourists transporting lava and pumice from the park. They made sure to mention, prior to arrival at the lava fields, that the goddess Pele, whose name in Hawaiian means 'molten lava', whose wrath is felt in volcanic eruptions, and who reportedly dwells in the crater of Kilauea, would bring bad luck to anyone who took a rock from the park (which is, coincidentally, a federal crime). The popular souvenir suddenly went from a fond remembrance of the vacation to

Hawaii, and a trophy of stealthy conquest for the mantle piece, to a cursed relic of trepidation and awe. Trepidation and awe are not always a deterrent; many people pay good money to watch horror flicks at the cinema, so as to wallow in it. But over time (most likely: after something bad happened) people started to want the cursed thing out of the house—every year the postal service on Hawaii started to handle thousands of pounds of rocks in packages addressed to 'postmaster', or to Queen Pele herself, from former visitors who may have, as happens in life, experienced some incidence of otherwise un-attributable misfortune. Though it is likely that others have kept their lava and pumice, and find the accursedness amusing. As William James, father of American psychology, saw in 1902 in *The Varieties of Religious Experience: A Study in Human Nature*, "Ideas efficacious for some people, prove inefficacious for others."

The Not-Too-Small Matter of Cigars Sigmund Freud, notorious cigar smoker, and ~~nefarious~~ well-known psychologist responsible for promoting the curse of seeing innuendo in everyday things, is sometimes quoted as having said, "Sometimes a cigar is just a cigar." It is unlikely he ever said it, but the degree of innuendo cast (in a petard-hoisting stylee) by this quote, is 'gob-stopping'. Once heard, it becomes impossible to ever see a picture of Sigmund Freud smoking a cigar the same way again. The situation has its origin in *The International Journal of Psycho-Analysis* of 1922 (Volume 3, Part 4). Sigmund Freud is, notably, credited as director of the journal, on the cover. In that volume is an article by Eric Hiller stated that cigars can symbolize the penis, being cylindrical & tubular, with a hot red end, and emitting something of potency (in the cigar's case, that would be smoke and burning embers). The article also seems to suggest that people start smoking because of the phallic significance of the cigar, making the cigar a substitute for the penis (or mother's breast), which they, apparently, later in life, for some reason pine for.

For some, the general shape of a cigar may be trivial; for others, unmentionable. A colorful paper band from an exotic land might make it far more attractive than its monochrome brown normally commands, as it cues the imagination to far off places. For some, the waft of fresh tobacco right from the humidor is more pleasure than the smoke, but for the smoker the smoke may be almost auto-aromatic. But after being exposed to Volume 3, Part 4 of *The International Journal of Psycho-Analysis* of 1922, there would seem to be only one way to see a cigar while maintaining a state of innocence, and only one way to smoke a cigar with self-image intact—and that would be by not thinking of a Freudian cigar, and the journal article seems to taint them all. But what if the cigar is not the small, thin Trabucco that Sigmund Freud smoked (up to 20 a day—he preferred Don Pedro, but the Austrian government restricted such proclivities, at least at the time)? Does the innuendo apply equally to a stubby Petit Corona? To a slim, elegant 6 1/2 inch Lonsdale? To a bulging Perfecto? Or even to the enormous 8 1/2 inch Diadema?

Yes, they are all touched. A cigar can be any particular single cigar, but 'cigar' is also a category of things, with a wide girth. It's like putting all cigars, no matter their properties into a box: a cigar box, which is another category of things, encompassing the Boite Nature, Semi-Boite Nature, Dress Box, and Flat

Top—whether they are made of eucalyptus, mahogany, rosewood, or top choice Spanish cedar they still fit the category. And the cigar box is just one type of box in the category of things that are boxes. The idea of a box encompasses all existing boxes, as well as all possible imaginable boxes in the future, ranging from some box that has a clown in it that will pop out when you turn the crank, to your very own mailbox. Your very own mailbox is an actual, verifiable thing, but the *idea* of boxes has quite a range of expressions, including the latest Amazon box that came in the mail only to be stomped flat as a pancake and put into the recycling. The stomped-flat Amazon box is *not* a pancake, it is still thought of as a box, despite now being flatly un-box-like. To others also bringing their recycling to the receptacle, the idea of your Amazon box is simply 'cardboard'. Similarly, the idea of mailboxes encompasses all mailboxes, whether a mini-cubicle in a big grid in a downtown high-rise, or a rusty quonset-hutty-like aluminum plate hollow on a post by a soybean-flanked highway with a red flag that is either up, or down, or the hollowed-out chess piece in the barracks at Stalag 17.

Each Hummel figurine is also a thing of its own, with a goose etc., but still belongs to the broader category, of Hummel figurines, though they belong to a broader category of things that are are knick-knacks. Not just any knick-knack, but a category of knick-knack that is genuine, factory stamped, and purchased from a reputable knick-knack dealer. Figs are fruit, a category of thing that is tasty sweet and good for you. If a friend hands you a paper bag and says there is fruit in it, and inside there is a hairy red ball that looks more like a sea anemone than any fruit in your memory pantry, and your friend says it is a 'rambutan', you figure you can confidently slice it open and eat what's inside, even though what pops out when sliced looks like a glossy gelatinous egg. But your friend said it was a fruit, and you trust this particular friend. Munching into the rambutan, it is indeed sweet and tasty—fruity—like you anticipated. There was no way to tell it would be edible by merely looking at the hairy red ball or the egg-like insides. The expectation of yummy was there because your friend told you it was a fruit; both you and your friend have a similar idea of the properties that things in the category of 'fruit' have; and this particular person (one of the individuals fitting, for you, the category of 'friend') is reliable. A less decent friend might have given you a durian, which is also a fruit, but which has been described as tasting like a blend of chives, cheese, sewage, turpentine and rotting animal carcasses, which is why durians are banned from public subways and buses in Singapore. So, when in Singapore, be sure to ask your friend specifically what kind of fruit it is that is in the bag, before using public transport.

A 'category' is a thing that belongs to the category of things that are not things, but they make life easier—such that if a friend hands you a bag, you don't need to look inside. If a friend were to hand you a paper bag and say that there is a 'cosmic crisp' in there, you might consider taking it to a nuclear waste facility for disposal (unless you live in Seattle and are fully aware that the 'cosmic crisp' is the first varietal of apple ever developed in the state of Washington, in which case you would assume that what is in the bag is not radioactive, but is a fruit). It would be easier if your friend had mentioned the general category 'apple', instead of the narrower category, 'cosmic crisp'. As it is, there are over 7,500 different kinds of edible apple, and if there were no such thing as the category 'apple, we would have to start from scratch every time anew to figure out what one is (the texture is moderately firm, it is semi-plasticky but a rough spike sticks out the top, etc.) and every trip to the grocery store would take a month.

The benefit of categories of things is that they provide priming for the mind. The mind yearns to assign categorical attributes to any encountered thing so that it can be more quickly figured out, which makes the case of the tomato particularly frustrating: it technically being a fruit, not a vegetable. People are completely within their rights, despite science, to continue to view the tomato as a vegetable, because 'if it walks like a duck, etc.', and the same ought to be true of vegetables. Steven Pinker notes that each individual thing cannot, in terms of practical everyday functioning, afford to be viewed as a thing like no other—it is essential for navigating the world to be able to see the similarities in newly encountered things. Categorical knowledge helps us understand, in advance, how a newly-encountered thing might work, or (generally true for the category of crawly things) if it is to be avoided. We naturally associate things with similar aspects or dimensions (e.g., rocks; figs), until proven otherwise—the pitfall being stereotypes and prejudices. But Pinker adds that once you start sharply delineating the criteria for a category, some things that should fit don't anymore. Categories that are fixed and rigid, get fuzzy around the edges, and may disassemble entirely. Categorizations are things we implicitly understand, but as with tomatoes, they can't ever fit any particular thing perfectly, because each particular thing has unique characteristics that don't fit other items in the category. Categories, like tomatoes, can get pretty squishy.

And 'squishy' is what ultimately befalls ideas. All ideas. With a computer, information uploaded today will be identical to the same file downloaded next year. With the human brain, ideas 'uploaded' today will be recalled tomorrow with vital words changed, in reverse order, in a different color, and wearing a party hat. In *The Runaway Brain: How Human Creativity Remakes the World* neuroscientist David Eagleman and artist Anthony Brandt detail what happens. The mind cannot help but twist & bend ideas like in a funhouse mirror, put them in a casserole and cook them up with other ideas plus spice, or take a hammer to them and bust them to pieces. Eagleman & Brandt say it is unclear precisely which biological substrates result in the 'bending', 'blending', and 'breaking' of ideas that the human mind performs relentlessly, but the sheer volume of neurons we have, the extensive lengths information has to travel through complex structures, and the possibility of spreading activation firing at not just a laser-strike warehouse, but entire conceptual industrial parks in a brain region, at the drop of a thought, seems to make a certain amount of variability (read: error) inevitable. Eagleman & Brandt explain that this is very different from nerve connections in insects. With insects connections are short and tight—inputs are more inerrantly connected to outputs—and this is why even mature fruit flies have no sense of humor.

The really good news, is that in humans all the data error—the mis-association, cross-pollination, pillage, plunder and data demolition—this is the stuff of creativity and innovation. Ideas morph, hairstyles morph, art galleries morph, puns happen—it's as if monkeys were in charge of the switchboards. To use a rock as a tool to smash open a coconut, you first have to imagine what happens when a rock hits a coconut, and the mind concocts things to do with rocks because it just can't help itself. The tombola of colliding ideas, along with the smorgasbord of combinatorial possibilities, leads to Edison's light bulb.

Thankfully, only a tiny fraction of the calculating and 'thinking' that the brain is doing pops into awareness at any particular time. The brain is a bubbling cauldron of unconscious learning, synthesizing and problem-solving, and only those things most pressing, most salient for a body to know tend to rise to the level of conscious awareness. This is why it can be particularly productive to take a break when working on a task. The brain actually continues to work on tasks while the conscious mind is washing the dishes. And while washing, or drying, an idea can suddenly pop into awareness that is an optimal solution.

'Priming' the mind is done by simply confronting a problem. An answer might not come right away, and attention shifts to other things, but a solution might suddenly pop into mind when the challenge is engaged again, or just 'out of the blue'. Priming the mind also orients understandings—for instance, after drinking cocktails in a convertible, the phrase 'tops down, bottoms up' is readily understood in its true context, instead of something wholly inappropriate. Priming—just by thinking a thought—also heightens future attention to what one has previously attended to—which is why advertisers advertise. It can also happen that when going to a thrift shop, special attention is given to Hummel figurines, depending upon what one has been reading.

Priming can also lead to errors of 'over-recognition' like—after study of comparative religions—seeing the Buddha in a piece of toast. Professor of Cognitive Philosophy Andy Clark suggests that the 'buzzing leg' phenomenon that some people experience follows upon the advent of cellphones in the pocket. People are used to the buzzing of pocket phones, and will then sense a buzzing at times when there is no phone there, as they are 'primed' to interpret the bottom-up input of random sensory events as a buzzing top-down telephone. Dr. Clark performed an experiment, where he primed subjects listening to pure, random white noise to see if they could hear Bing Crosby singing *White Christmas* subtly in the background. Many subjects did indeed report hearing Bing Crosby singing *White Christmas*, although there was actually no Bing Crosby singing *White Christmas* on the tape. A critique of the study might be that it is within the range of physical possibility for random white noise to arrange itself in such a way that it would coincidentally sound like Bing Crosby singing *White Christmas*, just as monkeys on keyboards if given enough time would eventually randomly type the entire works of William Shakespeare, though Dr. Clark's method was sound.

The opposite of hearing *White Christmas* when there is no *White Christmas* playing, is the inability to recognize *White Christmas* even when it is playing. Isabelle Peretz of the Massachusetts Institute of Technology reports the case of an individual who lost the ability to recognize music, including all her favorite songs. She could still recognize the lyrics to her favorite songs, and her recognition of other sounds, including speech, remained normal, but she lost the ability to 'name that tune', suggesting that musical tunes are handled in the mind in a specific warehouse, to which one can lose the key. Language is also warehoused in discrete areas, such that it is possible to lose all your ability to speak a native language, spoken since infancy, but still speak your high school French. Another variation is being able to only speak one's native language some days, and being able to only speak a foreign language on other days. Another possibility is following a stroke, speaking your native language with a foreign accent—for instance, you try to converse normally, but, for better or worse, you sound like the Swedish chef on The Muppets.

Oliver Sacks observed that our daily lives are wholly dependent upon memory, though sometimes this doesn't become apparent until someone suddenly loses an aspect of it (Sacks adds that if you lose *all* of it, there will no longer be a *you* there to know you lost it). From what to do when the alarm clock rings to what to nosh from the fridge before bed, memory is running routines and subroutines. All through the day memories, through dispositions and images, are constantly kicked into gear by just the most fragmentary reminders, nearly all of it happening outside the conscious awareness that is but the tip of our cognitive iceberg.

For What It's Worth   Oscar Wilde once said that a particular type of person knows, ". . . the price of everything, but the value of nothing." That may be too cynical a view: the price of something if it sells, is a clear estimation of value. If a banana sells for $120,000 then that is undeniably how much it was worth to someone, and if a thing at that price is coveted by more people, the price goes up even further. People assign value to everything, and although you might not pay a single cent for a rock, you might still value it enough to pick it up and put it in your pocket, until you begin to fear that Queen Pele values it more. All living beings are constant active day traders in the diurnal public market that is survival and well-being.

Antonio Damasio in *Self Comes to Mind* observes that 'value' is at the core of how the brain operates—actuarial calculation of losses, gains, and risks are a prominent feature of our mental circuitry, and assignment of value a virtual obsession. It goes back to the primordial architecture of life regulation, designed not just to maximize chance of survival, but to also enhance quality of life, well-being. The brain has feeling input from the body: discomfort vs. comfort. craving vs. satisfaction—then uses every available mechanism of calculation and innovation to maximize the latter in the aforementioned pairs. Things that enhance existence and flourishing earn higher value, and those that don't, don't.

A particular object does not have one set value; it will vary depending upon circumstance. A turkey baster in the drawer on the 4th of July is something that gets in the way, but on a certain day in November if the rapscallions failed to return it from the wading pool it becomes 'my kingdom for a turkey baster.' A thing also has value across different dimensions. An apple has nutritional value, as well as pleasing flavor, but can also lend a sense of flourishing and abundance when viewed in a still life Caravaggio oil on canvas, with appreciation of the shadings in the frame and the ripeness of fruit leading to awe for the unique perspective and masterly skill of the artist—all delicious in their own right, and a celebration of well-being, particularly if it is possible to own the painting, though usually the laminated placemat from the museum shop will have to do.

Tulip bulbs also have different dimension of value, as epitomized by 'Tulip Mania' of the Dutch Golden Age when the bulb was both the promise of a bloom, and a form of speculative currency. The tulip bulb bubble lasted from late 1636 until February 6, 1637; during the market frenzy a single bulb could sell for more than 100 times what a skilled laborer made in a year. History has scratched its head at what seem to be insane bulb prices, but the Dutch had not all suddenly become maniacs. It is completely sane to buy a thing at one price and sell it at a higher price—just as it is perfectly normal to want to acquire things of beauty and exclusivity, that bring joy. It was not the skilled laborers paying 100 times their annual wage for the bulby baubles, it was people with gaggles of Guilders who bought them. Prices for particular bulbs rose because specific varietals of tulip developed speckles and stripes that were unique, and it became fashionable to purchase these as a luxury, just as someone might purchase art. Tulips only bloom for one to two weeks, but it made wealthy merchants and aristocrats happy—a happiness that money could buy. Just the idea of being able to afford paying a small fortune for an ephemeral bloom likely made them even happier—a flowering reminder of flourishing success.

Once the tulip bulb bubble burst there were undoubtedly

investors left with product impossible to flog profitably, and poisonous to eat (although the petals of grown tulips can be used as a salad garnish), but that's day trading for you. Dutch 'Tulip Mania' was a simple case of supply and demand, similar to Beanie Babies in the 1990s, when a $5 plush toy could resell for over $1000 before the plush toy lost its luster (some traders were reported to have lost as much as $100,000 when the Beanie Baby bubble burst, and unlike tulip petals, they could not be used as a salad garnish).

Steven Pinker in *How the Mind Works* points out that not only do tastes change, but a quick twist in the idea about a thing can decimate its value. In other news: a painting found to be created by a student of the master, and not the master himself, will suddenly plummet in value. And if it is found to be a forged copy, it will drop from sky high to zero, and the feeling it evokes can shift from aesthetic pleasure to horror. Is it still pretty? Likely. But not six-figures pretty. So it goes in the value jungle of human culture. Still, some things, like a lush, colorful, bounteous garden tend to always be attractive; a scruffy, scraggly patchy garden with rotten vegetables, just the opposite.

A thing that never seems to lose its allure, is money. Money is the idea of value, incarnate. It is incarnated into metal slugs and sheets of rectangular paper. Small children, as soon as they are old enough to not eat slugs and paper, when told, quickly learn to understand that the coins and bills have currency far beyond the value of other pieces of paper. Three-year-olds even get excited when they get stickers for potty skills, and not much later can comprehend that a piece of paper with a ten on it is worth much more than one with a one on it, despite being the exact same size and weight.

The idea of ten dollars as embodied by a piece of paper with the ten on it is something that all of us have learned and mutually agreed upon to be worth ten times the piece of paper with the one on it. This, despite the fact, that the government can print all it wants of the ones and tens and hundreds. The gambit only works because everyone shares the same idea about the thing: that the one with the ten on it can get you an ice cream or two, but the one with the one on it can't. The system works because we are all hardwired to trade in ideas; it is the idea of value that is represented by something as insubstantial as a piece of paper, something instantly understood and shared across all human cultures.

Still, there are things that can have more value than any amount of money to an individual, as they are rooted in a far more primal biology. They can relegate even the most florid and abundant garden, the most expansively sublime front porch, or the Caravaggio placemats to obscurity. In the words of Marcel Proust: "Love is a striking example of how little reality means to us ... we may remember a particular atmosphere, but it is because girls were smiling in it." William James saw the same happening, for chickens: "To the broody hen, this notion would probably seem monstrous: that there should be a creature in the world, to whom a nest full of eggs was not utterly fascinating, and precious, and the never-to-be-too-much-sat-upon object, which it is to her."

Things Glorious Things Pets are popular things, and by far the most popular pets in term of numbers sold are aquarium fish. One of the very most popular aquarium fish is the guppy. Guppies are popular because they have flamboyant fins with fantastic color that make for much flash in the tank thanks to their frisky nature. The males are actually the more colorful, and they use their finery and flair to attract females. Female guppies are attracted foremost to the males with the brightest colors, particularly the color orange, along with 'size'. However, when a female guppy observes a less naturally attractive, less colorful, less sizable male being courted by another female, the female guppy will forget about male guppies of superior color and size, and then covet the other-courted guppy. This phenomenon, known as 'mate-choice copying' has also been documented in the mouse, the quail, and the human being. In the case of humans, even the grass seems to be greener (like guppy fins that are oranger) on the other side of the fence, over at the Joneses' place. But with humans, the phenomenon is not limited to potential mates. It includes things—things that are coveted and possessed—and unlike squirrels who are forced to bury their most prized possessions (~25% of which are stolen by other squirrels, and another ~50% they fail to retrieve) the typical American home houses ~300,000 items.

The phenomenon of human valuing, coveting, and possessing was dissected extensively by Thorsten Bunde Veblen in 1899. Veblen had a humble background, growing up the son of Norwegian immigrants in Cato, Wisconsin, which is not far from Manitowoc. His origins outside the mainstream of American society, as northern Wisconsin sometimes is, gave him a unique take on social structure and consumerism once he went east to study philosophy and economics at Johns Hopkins and Yale, leading him to eventually invent the term 'conspicuous consumption'. Veblen traced people's pride in their things back to the booty from hunting and war in days of yore. The pelts, the fangs, the shrunken heads—these items brought esteem for the victors, from others in the community. The possession of such trophies conferred 'honour' on the holder, much like the T-ball trophies that all participants receive today. Following the era when hunter-gatherers and warring tribes set the popular standard of success, Veblen found that, "Property is still of the nature of trophy, but, with the cultural advance, it becomes more and more a trophy of successes scored in the game of ownership". Veblen determined that simply having lots of things became the new standard for community esteem. The things that used to confer honor from conquest in hunting and war, turned into things that conferred honor by being bought at the store. But Veblen saw that once "the possession of property becomes the basis of popular esteem", nothing was ever enough. Once a desired standard of ownership status was attained, it then became insufficient, or trumped by the Joneses next door, resulting in the "desire of every one to excel every one else in the accumulation of goods." According to Veblen, excelling in wealth conferred power—but only when it was obvious to others, and not stuffed in a mattress.

If Veblen was correct and not merely jealous, one lingering question is whether there is inherent value in things that are valuable, or whether the value of things is dependent upon their Jonesian keeping-upness. One piece of paper is worth more than another because cultures determine it is. An avocado green kitchen used to raise the value of a home, but then later significantly lowered it. Antiques were once rare treasures with television programs dedicated to assessing their value, until the power of IKEA magically turned them back into creaky old furniture. But nothing says rat-race culture-chase more than clothing. To be more precise: fashion. Veblen saw a constantly churning cultural code determining what fashion is currently suitable, with, "departures from the code," being, "offensive to our taste." In other words, "We readily, and for the most part with utter sincerity, find those things pleasing that are in vogue." Take bonnets. Very few people take bonnets any more, and if it weren't for the likes of *Little House on the Prairie* modern civilization might never know their striking charm. Veblen observed: "A fancy bonnet of this year's model unquestionably appeals to our sensibilities today much more forcibly than an equally fancy bonnet of the model of last year; although . . . it would, I apprehend, be a matter of the utmost difficulty to award the palm for intrinsic beauty to the one rather than to the other of these structures."

An 1898 bonnet to Veblen was far less appealing than the 1899 model, though to look at them on Google Images today, everyone is sure to find a favorite—perhaps with more aesthetic objectivity than the late 19th Century perspectives so potently swayed by what is fashionable in the moment. Still, in our times few would wear even the most fetching of them to tomorrow's cocktail party. Fashion, as in any particular bonnet, shifts hard and fast, often from winter to spring to summer to fall, though the broad category of things that is 'fashion' is always in fashion—a hot commodity, with the crest of the fashion wave garnering top price. Any particular raspberry beret may be 'honorific' to the wearer in a particular culture one week, then horrific when the next weekly Top 40 comes out, but the force in human existence that is 'style' never goes out of style. A guppy's size and vibrancy in color reflects aspects of its biological fitness, hence its suitability as a mate. But guppy's are stuck with what they got stuck with. Humans go to the store and pick up accoutrement with accents and insignia that changes their shape, and how they are viewed. The peacock goes to great lengths to fan out the feathers, but human feathered finery can be had at the haberdashers, to convey signals about a person's vitality, savvy, charms and triumphs with an alacrity and potency that would make a guppy blush.

Fashion is instant information, and a female guppy's interest in a less vibrantly haberdashed specimen represents a shortcut to potentially better information. Others have had experiences we haven't, and perhaps they know things we don't. We can't each be expected to know on our own about everything that is worthwhile, and what might have significant value—so we keep our eye on others. If you are in a foreign supermarket and you want to know what wine is good, watch what locals reach for—or choose a wine where there is a receding gap in the shelf space. If you are out on a Saturday night and want to know who the hottest fish in the sea is, check out who the other fish are flippering after.

But we don't necessarily need to surveil—we can just ask. Ask the haberdasher what's in vogue, or the shop's wine buyer for the de rigueur cabernet, or say, "Say, what is it exactly you see in that ugly guppy you are swimming upstream with?" If you are traveling in a small town in America and want to know where the post office is, you can just ~~ask a gas station attendant~~ google it. Language is a shortcut to value: what path to take, what Pinot Grigio goes with tulip petals. We learn and share ideas of value with others, and although this can lead to the occasional fad, fads are fab fun. Herd behavior pays off most of the time, and even if you wind up stuck with a couple dozen extra un-eBay-able Beanie Babies—they're still cute.

Whatever the history and the oblique motivations behind the warm associations people have with the things they have—whether they are useful, or somehow attractive, or make you top banana—things provide constant reflection of value, and are alive with associations and feeling. Even things that are little more than remembrances of value past are still a warm bath.

Halftime Report

Color Commentator: "So, narrative voice of Section I: your initial approach comes off as slapdash, half-cocked, more than a little daft. Why did you take such a tangential approach to the matters at hand, and pepper your expressions with groan-worthy asides?"

Narrative Voice of Section I: "It's because if you go straight for the end-zone on the first play from scrimmage, the defense will have their dander up. Instead, we did a halfback fake, and the pass option, followed by an end-around, and finally the Statue of Liberty play, to keep them off guard."

Color Commentator: "Uff da. Narrator of Section II, you did not exactly cover yourself with ice-cream-sprinkles of glory. Instead, you dragged us all through the cocoa. Why did you choose to bunny about like that?"

Narrative Voice of Section II: "It's because we needed to run down the clock."

Color Commentator: "Understandably. And narrative voice of section III: what the heck?!"

Narrative Voice of Section III: "Hey! That was good stuff!"

Color Commentator: "To sum it all up: when we are awake and alert, our minds receive a nonstop flowing stream of perception from the external world, though the world is not experienced directly—it is first translated into coded electrical impulses, then converted into mental images (e.g., sound, vision, touch) that we are predisposed to make sense of in ways that are useful to us as organisms that want to survive and thrive in the niche we inhabit."

Narrative Voice of Section I: "Something like that, kinda, and you're leaving out a whole bunch of stuff."

Color Commentator: "And the things we image in our minds do actually represent real things outside ourselves in the world, though there might be more to them than we can sense, and most of our experience is shaped by 'top-down' predictions and projections anyways, that, at times, can wholly supersede or replace the objects we believe are in our actual perception, so we use 'real life' anchors to guide our otherwise less-than-rooted imagination, but if elements of the sensory stream are absent, the mind then fills in the scenery to create a seamless theater in the mind, similar to what is happening when we dream at night—beyond that, we have no way of knowing to what extent people, let alone other species, experience the same things, though since humans can talk, they can sometimes compare notes."

Narrative Voice of Section II: "You are barking up the right tree. But you are the wrong dog."

Color Commentator: "And everything we encounter has relative life-value, conveyed to us through feelings, such that all our perceptions are necessarily imbued with feeling, and all our experience fully conditioned by feelings, which we can sometimes shift by changing our ideas about things. How is it then, that things really are as they seem?"

Narrative Voice of Section III: "Things really are as they seem, because it's the reality you have; it's what you know, and what you have to work with—it's as real as anything else. You can use scientific gadgets to learn more about things, to change your idea of things, but then there you still are. Then you can read. Talk to people. Compare notes. And there you are again—it's the best we can do. Objective evidence and certitude are doubtless very fine ideals to play with, but where on this moonlit and dream-visited planet are they found? William James said that. In 1896. All you can know is your idea of things, because when you really come down to it, the Imagination is not a State: it is the Human Existence itself. William Blake wrote that in 1810. He even capitalized the nouns."

IV. THINGS: A TO Z

A: [see: Apple]

A: A Aaaaa Bcalvy   'A Aaaaa Bcalvy 24 Hour Carpet Fire Carpet Water Damage Specialist' was the sixth listing in the 1993 Pacific Bell Smart Yellow Pages. Despite the name beginning with the most initial 'a's among all submissions, Pac Bell's unique alphabetization algorithm placed 'A Aaaaa Bcalvy' (along with 'A Ace Pest & Termite Control' and 60 businesses with names beginning with 'A-1') behind top-listed 'A&A Mortgage Company of Westlake Village', in the 4 lb. phone book. [see: Alphabet]

A: Acetate Overlay Book Pages   Some tourist picture books of historical places, like the Roman Forum, Pompeii, and the Parthenon, have flip pages that are semi-transparent acetate overlays. On the background page will be an image of the Roman Forum as the enchanting ruin it is now. Flipping over the partly opaque, partly transparent acetate overlay page covers the ruinous bits with images of the Forum from back in the time when it was functional, orderly and not nearly as interesting. Clear areas on the acetate overlay page leave the surviving features on the background page intact (as they are seen today), while the overlay page imposes an opaque filter of what you would have seen before the Forum became an animal grazing pasture in the Middle Ages. The shell of a ruined room in Pompeii, on the other hand, when the overlay lays in, will come alive with the vivid colors of fresh frescoes and mosaics, before the summary eruption and excavation.

Opaque and semi-opaque acetate page overlays are also used in books about natural science to illustrate the discovery and wonder behind everyday things. In the 2004 volume *Mister Seahorse* by Eric Carle, cleverly camouflaged sea creatures hidden behind an opaque curtain of seaweed, coral reef, and a rock are uncovered by pulling back the acetate overlay. In Jan Stradling's illustrative *The Wonders Inside Bugs and Spiders* acetate pages conceal, then reveal, the hidden workings of insect innards.

The flip book of human perception does just the same. Two individuals standing at the same bus stop, and gazing ahead in order to avoid each others' gaze, might be sensorily processing the very same scene—the inputs could be virtually identical—but may observe very different things. The acetate overlay book page in each individual's mind filters out some elements in the scene, while bringing others to the fore. The scene each person perceives has individual color and atmosphere; some things are camouflaged while in plain sight, and others jump out from the tableau like magic, similar to the wonders in *Mister Seahorse*.

Cognitive scientist Alexandra Horowitz sought to compare her perceptions on a familiar neighborhood walk with that of eleven individuals with different orientations and expertise, leading to a wealth of new dimensions and surprises for her in On Looking: Eleven Walks with Expert Eyes. Among the many vivid insights, a geologist saw what he saw as a contrast between biological and mineral; a medical educator saw indications of people's jobs, religion, and medical afflictions in how people walked; a social worker who happened to be blind was highly attuned to the flow of wind as it courses around buildings; a sound engineer was sensitive to the noises things make when they are wet vs. dry; and her own toddler child showed particular interest in how objects all around felt and, uhh, tasted.

Clearly background knowledge, specialization, and interest make certain things stand out in a scene, as do expectations. When you eat an apple you expect apple, and might overlook worm. When you walk on the carpet, you expect cut pile fiber, not Lego. The arbiter is attention—what is attended to, what is salient, what is important in any situation, because if everything in a scene jumped out at you, you'd be floored. As William James intimated in *The Principles of Psychology*, "The art of being wise is the art of knowing what to overlook," and, "the function of ignoring, of inattention, is as vital a factor in mental progress as the function of attention itself."

One situation when everything is in plain view but nothing at all registers is the 'thousand yard stare'. In the case of the 'thousand yard stare' a person is looking dead ahead, eyes fully working, retina and visual processing areas active as ever, and nothing has form or valence. This happens in situations like just realizing the wallet is missing. The mind is focused entirely on searching the memory banks for most recent instances of the thing that is wallet—whether it was in the pocket or purse, or at the last shop, or left at home in the other pants. The overlay appliqué in the case of the 'thousand yard stare' works like a gray camera lens filter, with a bit of blur. In that moment, only information barely essential for navigating the environment is processed, half-wittingly at that, while heading zombie-like through the shopping day crowds back to the Marks & Spencer.

Attention can also wax and wane. Driving down an unfamiliar road looking for the little thrift shop with the Hummel figurines, as block by commercial block passes, with stores of every ilk but thrift, attention is heightened, and time slows to a crawl, as every sign and shop window is examined so that the goal won't be overlooked till the thrift shop is found. Focus is sharp; every building shape and sign registers. Driving back—although just as physically awake as on the approach—the very same stretch of road and driving distance all becomes incidental stage scenery and goes by lickety-split.

Another mental overlay on a scene is mood, with joy enhancing color and brightness, and fear or sorrow often casting a pall. Another is belief. If you don't believe in faeries, then you might not see any faeries. If you do believe in faeries, then every rustle in the bush sparkles with promise, even if you don't see any faeries. If you go to Liverpool, and you believe all Liverpudlians are alike, you don't have to pay attention to any of the nuance or discrepancy in their actual behavior.

Beliefs can impose a fixed and sometimes predominant overlay on a landscape. They can provide orientation and structure in what otherwise can be a wild and wooly world, bringing ease. They can plaster over things that would otherwise pose challenges and need to be reconciled, requiring undue time, effort, and mental gymnastics. Belief systems can save time and confusion, but if the fixed features in the overlay begin to opaquely fill the page, they can utterly obscure the scene.

Another type of overlay, a social filter, can be illustrated by the difference between having a coffee stain on your shirt vs. having spinach in your teeth. If you have spinach in your teeth, you might notice others staring, perhaps with a wry smile, or even a giggle, but you happily carry on talking as if all is just peachy. If, on the other hand, you have a coffee stain on your shirt, you think that people are looking at you funny because of the coffee stain on your shirt, even if they have not actually seen the coffee stain on your shirt, and are not actually looking at you funny—or, they have not seen the coffee stain on your shirt, and are indeed looking at you funny, but it is because of the spinach in your teeth, not the spot on your shirt. You can go to the Louvre and see the Mona Lisa, and even though your conscious mind knows that the painting was done in 1503, you still get the feeling that her wry smirk is from seeing the coffee stain on your shirt.

Whether acetate overlay book pages are more opaque or more transparent; clear or tinted; cluttered or clean; the will flip again from moment to moment, and vary very much from person to person. In the words of William James, "It would probably astound each of us beyond measure to be let into his neighbor's mind and to find how different the scenery was there from that of his own."

A: Advertising   Advertising is the process of making the brain think about something being sold, and then pairing that something with aspects, objects, and feelings of a positive nature that the mind is already plenty happy about. The essential dimensions are:

* **Let people know the thing exists**: otherwise people might not know that there is such a thing. A thing doesn't sell well if people don't know it exists. Or, they might know it exists, but have no idea what to do with it. For instance, those who visited the baths in ancient Rome might have paid no attention to a tube made of asbestos, roughly one cubit long. But if they had seen advertisements, they would know that it is a 'bastardius', used to slather bathers with olive oil, and might then want to buy one for home use. If they were clever, and worked with a savvy ancient ad agency, they could in turn market the very same device for use in the kitchen. As it so happens, the bastardius was the ancient forerunner of the turkey baster.

* **Associate the thing with other nice things**: as William James found in 1899: "Any object not interesting in itself may become interesting through becoming associated with an object in which an interest already exists." That is why a product such as a turkey baster benefits by being featured in scenes of handsome & pretty happy people in bikinis laughing and drinking Mai Tais while playing beach volleyball. The turkey baster can also be given allure by pairing it with disposition-igniting adjectives in the ad copy, such as, 'genuine', 'famous', 'adorable', 'award-

winning', 'captivating', 'no-fuss', and 'state-of-the-art' turkey baster.

* **Activate people's senses when they are in the presence of the thing:** Stores use subliminal sensual strategies to stimulate sales, and it has been estimated that as much as 95% of spontaneous purchasing decisions result from subtle scents, canny colors, and arty arrangement. One of the first to recognize the benefit was Henry Selfridge, whose 1909 London department store had the perfumes placed by the entrance, both to enchant, as well as to cover the reek of horse-appled Oxford Street outside. Fast forward to grocery stores that put bright fruits up front to enliven the mind, along with the chicken roasting on a spit to get people salivating. Then there is the home improvement store enlivened with the odor of fresh cut wood where none is being cut; every nook and cranny of an entire cineplex redolent with popcorn, though they sell pizza too but you don't smell that; a car that uses a microphone in the engine and plays the sound through the stereo system to make the car sound revvier; the coconut aroma by the swimwear to transport the mind back to sunscreen slathered at the seaside; chocolaty whiffs at vending machines; christmassy smells at Christmas. It should come as no surprise that stores play the style of music favored most by the demographic they purvey to, but a wine shop owner might find it strategic to know that oenophiles are more likely to choose French or German wine, depending upon whether French or German music is playing in the background. It doesn't stop at the front door—the scents, whether real or creative chemical, are pumped out into the street or mall from the stores: the coffee essence from the café, the waxy cinnamon

waft from the candle store, the intoxicating scent of roasting nuts even when all the nuts are factory packaged.

* Make sure any modified thing is consistent with people's idea of the thing: In From Those Wonderful Folks Who Gave You Pearl Harbor, Jerry Della Femina, one of Madison Avenue's original 'admen' with a capital 'M', tells how Johnson & Johnson created a first-aid cream that was gentle to the skin and went on smooth as hand cream, with no pain or irritation. People wouldn't use it. So they put a bit of alcohol into the first-aid cream such that when it was applied to a cut it had a slight burn. People's idea of first-aid cream included the sting; without that sensation it was more like the idea of inert hand lotion. The admen assigned to the campaign for the first first-aid cream that doesn't sting had to go back to the drawing board. Della Femina also tells about a cake mix where all you had to do was add water. Market research showed that people did not like it. So they changed the cake mix so that you add water but also have to crack an egg into it. Then it was fine. People's idea of making a cake at home requires more than just adding water, it needs an egg too.

A: **Alphabet**   [see: A Aaaaa Bcalvy]

A: **Amoeba**   Already taken.

A: **Amoeba, second attempt**   An amoeba is a single-cellular creature adrift in an amorphous sea of threats and temptations, with only the most raw and primitive sense of where to go next and what to pursue, like an introvert at a cocktail party.

A: **Aplomb**   Small purplish fruit.

A: Appendix   The last entry in a book, under normal circumstances.

A: Apple

> 'A' is for apple everyone knows; for alphabet listings should never propose to upset traditions of patterns familiar; 'cause things unexpected are things that'll kill yer! Homeostasis demands familiarity—upsetting apple carts leads to despairity!

'A' is for apple and apple ought to be the very first entry in the alphabetical listing of things. Sometimes alphabet books begin with 'A is for aardvark' but that is when writers are trying to be clever. There are theological argumentations well supporting this precept from the 'B' as in Bible.

A: Armadillo   Alphabetically subordinate to the aardvark, but with superior leaping ability.

B: Bonnet   The flat layer of metal, with a hinge and support stick (bonnet strut), that can be raised to provide access to the engine of a car, to check & replace fluids and perform repair work (British usage).

B: Book   The physical thing that is a book can differ in height, width, thickness, and hardness from other books. Book covers differ too, though you can't tell a book by them. The primary category of physical book are hardback and paperback, though these are being superseded by books that are made up of bits and bytes, such that the physical thing that is a book is now an endangered species. If, in the future, there are no bookstores nor physical books, than all that will be left is the pure idea of a book, which will consist of ideas conveyed through patterns of light and darkness to form symbols of letters, numbers, and punctuation in electronic media.

There are two main kinds of patterns of light and darkness forming symbols to represent ideas: fiction and non-fiction. Books that purport to be fiction often describe real life places and objects, and pretend not to describe real life people for legal reasons though they often do. Both fiction and non-fiction are on a sliding scale. Books that purport to be non-fiction swear up and down that events in them are true, but memory is faulty, each writer interprets events differently, and the imagination formulates the entire non-fiction book in a way that will never be identical to any other non-fiction creation—most likely wildly different. Marcel Proust suggested that it doesn't matter what the writer of the book intended anyway, because the meaning of the patterns of light and darkness are ultimately the invention of the person decoding them. To Proust the symbols are an optical aid that helps anyone scanning the symbols read one's own self, and discover aspects that might never been seen in one's own self; the truth of the book, for Proust, is what is recognized as resonating from the book within the reader.

B: **Boot**   The part of a car on the opposite end from the bonnet (British usage; in American English it is called a trunk; in Indian English it is called a dickey). Unlike the bonnet, the boot cover does not house an engine; the boot is typically empty except for emergency equipment, sports equipment, spare tire, groceries in transit, hostages & dead bodies (Hollywood usage), and on boot-sale days it holds merchandise for display.

B: **Brass Rubbings**   In Victorian England it became popular to visit churches with tombs on the floor of wealthy, important, or holy people covered with a stone or brass plaque engraved with the image of the noble person beneath. The plaques took less room, were cheaper, and were less likely to have the nose chipped off as invaders and vandals often did than alabaster figures or statues. Created roughly between 1250 and 1650, the often elaborately engraved plaques of praying clergy, knights in full regalia, or coats of arms were carved in relief, so that visitors would cover the plaque with a long sheet of paper (many were life-sized) and rub the surface of the paper with a waxy crayon, then take the sketchy impression of Thomas Goodryke, Bishop of Ely or Alianore de Bohun, Duchess of Gloucester home and hang it on the wall. Whether crayon, wax, chalk, or graphite, the brass rubbing made by the average person would be faint in spots, miss detail, be subject to errant marks, be slightly distorted by the angle of approach of the arm and subject to error if the paper shifts. Still, the gist of Lady Maud de Cromwell would be generally recognizable, which makes brass rubbings an apt if sketchily strained metaphor for human memory. It is the gist of things that is retained in memory. Details not so much. Details of a thing in memory, where the gist is well understood, can sometimes have the quality of a brass rubbing that was dropped in a muddy puddle by the curb on the way out of the church then run over by a horse-drawn wagon, before the dogs got at it.

B: **Breadbox**   Physical breadboxes were once a common household item but have lost favor because they are bulky, and the advent of preservatives, plastic bagging, and storing bread in the freezer have speeded their obsolescence. Breadboxes will keep unsliced, no-preservative loaves fresh and nicely crusty longer than other methods, and keeps them away from the cat, but there are many people alive today who have never seen a breadbox. Still, even if they will never use a breadbox to box bread, they need to have an idea of a breadbox for those times when they are asked, "Is it bigger than a breadbox?" Those who have never seen a breadbox then imagine a loaf of bread with a box around it, and try to get by answering the question based upon that construal, and hope they don't get called out for misrepresentation once the game of '20 Questions' is over.

B: **Bumper Saucers**   A mix of bumper car, flying saucer, and air hockey that served as a ride at Disneyland between 1961 and 1966. Leaning one way or the other in the saucer would allow the air jets to send you careening into other saucer riders of your choice. If sitting bolt upright, the saucer would hop up and down. The ride was costly to operate, required excessive maintenance, and only a limited number of saucer riders could ride each day, so the ride was discontinued. Bumper saucers are not much of a metaphor for anything.

C: **Cap'N Crunch**   Designed to mimic the flavor of butter & brown sugar on rice, Cap'N Crunch was the first breakfast cereal to use an oil coating on the cereal in the production process. Since its invention in 1963, Cap'N Crunch has become more popular than the idea of butter & brown sugar on rice.

C: **Chicken, bawking like a**   Most people who find themselves bawking like a chicken, but don't really understand why, have been sitting in the audience of a stage hypnotist who attempted an hypnotic induction of the entire audience, with the chicken bawker being one of the very few in the audience highly responsive to the induction. The hypnotist watches audience members react to the hypnotic induction, and how forcefully they start swatting at the fly the hypnotist says is buzzing around their head when there is no fly, while others (those not very susceptible to hypnotic induction) are sitting there thinking the fly thing is silly. Those who were most perturbed by the imaginary fly are then invited onstage to bawk like a chicken.

Individuals who have been hypnotized to the point of going up onstage have later said that they were well aware of their surroundings, felt alert, but at the same time responded to the commands of the hypnotist, including raising the arm when they were told it was being lifted by balloons on strings, and dropping the head when told their head felt very heavy. Hypnotic subjects, while still fully alert, may know the audience is present, and may even hear things audience members call out, but these things don't have valence—they don't register. If told to forget the number 3, and then told to count on their fingers out loud, they will say, "1 ... 2 ...." then be unable to say 3, even though they still have a perfectly good idea and understanding of the number 3. The knowledge is there, but the behavior of saying '3' just doesn't happen for them. When then told to stand up, flap arms, and bawk like a chicken, they do so, while at the same time realizing that the whole thing is silly, and there is a possibility they may be making a fool of themselves. They don't feel as if in a trance, nor in an altered state, they just do it, as if that just happens to be the thing to do. If told by the hypnotist not to remember certain things happening at the time, they won't focus attention on those things until perhaps later, when they are heading home, telling friends it was all an act, and weren't they convincing?

Hypnotism has been studied with brain scan technology, but there is no clear evidence of unusual brain activity in hypnosis. Instead, as Terhune, Cleereman, Raz & Lynn, detail in their study 'Hypnosis and Top-down Regulation of Consciousness' it appears top-down dispositions are kicking in hard, diverting attention to certain particular things that will determine thought & action (similar, in a way, to being in an auto accident when there is hyper focus just on what is vital). Top-down dispositions and mechanisms take focus even when 'bottom-up' perceptions are happening as always. Focus is not lost, instead the mind is hyper-focused on particular ideas and actions, with other elements in the situation fading into a far-less-meaningful background. Some individuals seem more prone to having this kind of strong top-down scenario take over their actions than others. There is also a significant social demand component in the chicken-bawking situation, with it also likely that some are more responsive to authoritative suggestion than others—just as some children will immediately shift their attention and behavior when their parents or teachers command them, while others may ~~bawk~~ balk, and then run around like chickens with their heads cut off.

C: Chinese Box   'Chinese box' refers to an idea that consists of a cluster of ideas, each embedded within one another, similar to the way categories contain sub-categories, that in turn contain individual items within the category. Some motion pictures have a Chinese box structure, where the end happens first, and different scenes then unfold to explain what happened in the end, which is at the beginning. A Chinese box, in addition to being an idea that is an elaborate scaffolding of ideas, can also be a thing: a box with other boxes embedded within one another, like Russian wooden Babushka dolls.

C: Cigar   Nothing to see here.

C: Cinema   The mind reels. [see: Movies]

C: Cookie   [see: Priming]

C: Clutter   Clutter consists of things that are not stored away that aren't pretty, don't evoke sweet associations, and don't serve any useful function in their current spot. A paperweight that is not holding down papers, and that will not be holding down papers anytime soon, and is not breathtakingly lovely, and has no wealth of fond memories associated with it, is clutter. At first clutter, when seen, is ignored, because that is the easiest thing to do, but when noticed often enough it collects layers of mental dust if not outright mental fungus. Mentally dusty or fungal clutter, over a long enough time, becomes radioactively annoying, though the radioactive annoyance never rises to the level of conscious awareness, because ignoring the clutter has developed into a well-entrenched habit.

C: Cookie-clutter   Crumbs.

C: Coffee   The idea of coffee ranges from hot water & extracted coffee bean to the, "Grande nonfat soymilk sugar-free syrup hazelnut nutmeg 8-pumps-vanilla cinnamon peppermint chocolate sauce caramel-drizzled no-foam extra-whip iced flappucino: hold the coffee please." Coffee beans range from the

Robusta varietal mass-produced on valley floors with a strong, bitter, sometimes rubbery flavor, to the many varieties of Arabica (e.g., Caturra, Catuai, Catimor et. al.) grown at high altitude and processed using either dry method (with natural core intact) or wet method (removing the cherry prior to washing). Arabica is sweeter with more aromatics than Robusta, and is used to produce such coffee drinks as the 'flat white', which tastes like Australia. Next time, for a change, when ordering a Venti 2% almond milk 6-pump hazelnut caramel-drizzled no-foam extra whip latte, why not try asking it be made with wet-processed raised-bed-dried Sigararutang Arabica cultivated between 1400 and 1600 meters in the Jambi province of Sumatra?

C: Collections of Things Can you ever have too much of a good thing? If it is 'too much', then, by definition, yes. Singing star Janet Jackson started collecting porcelain pigs, and when her fans found out, they inundated her with porcelain pigs, and after accumulating hundreds, she felt it was too much, and stopped collecting them. Elton John was reported to have over 250,000 pairs of sunglasses. Actress Penélope Cruz was reported to have a collection of over 500 coat hangers. Some might ask why [see: Y]. Beyond the thrill of the chase, the interesting places the hunt may lead, the fascination inherent in variety, the insights gained in pursuing thing-related knowledge, the conversations with other enthusiastic collectors, the easy relaxation of enjoying a pleasurable dalliance, the richness of nostalgia that develops over time to rekindle memories of treasure-hunting past, and the amusement & appreciation in reflective perusal of the collection, there would seem to be no rational reason.

C: **Core Self**   Core self, or core consciousness, according to Antonio Damasio is a state of being that complex creatures share, that might be described in practical terms as being present in the moment: like a frog on a lily pad alert for flies, or a human rocking in a chair on the front porch with a margarita, or the cat plopped down on the newspaper you are trying to read, licking its paws. Each of these creatures is aware of the environment, is aware of its own body, responds to subtle changes in the surroundings, and has a sense of being a living entity, with feelings and sensations, an active presence in the moment. Core consciousness is not about regretting life's mistakes, calculating the square root of 2, or making plans for Nigel. The navel is not even contemplated—it is free just to be an unexamined, non-judged, un-mentally-molested navel, probably not even a factor in awareness, having none of the sensory immediacy of the breeze on the hairs by the ears or the pursing of lips from the tartness of the lime—things also not judged, but part of core sensations felt in the moment. The thinking apparatus, from an internal dialogue perspective, might be dialed down to nil at times like these, but in antithesis to Descartes' dictum, "I think, therefore I am", Antonio Damasio makes clear in *Descartes' Error* that you nevertheless still are, even if you don't ponder on the matter.

D: **Dots, random**   Anyone can make a big symmetrical inkblot by pouring ink on a sheet of paper then folding in half, and opening it again so that there are matching images on both halves of the paper. But if there is too much ink, it will look like a giant dot. If you then ask people what it looks like to them, they are likely to tell you precisely that. If, instead, there is less ink, such that the ink runs in different directions forming lines and blotches, and you ask people what it looks like to them, and every one of them says, "a butterfly," then your inkblot would not have met the rigorous standards of ambiguity set by Hermann Rorschach, whose collection of ink blots were complex and detailed, but didn't look like anything in particular. People who viewed them each had an idea of just what the ink blots pictured, though each of the responses tended to be individual. The most common responses to the Rorschach inkblots, first published in 1921, involved humans or beasts, though the savvy respondent knew to skew the response toward nice and friendly, and avoid mention of things gruesome or bawdy. Otherwise, the shrink might get ideas.

Most people would agree that the Rorschach inkblots have an ominous, disturbing, even obscene quality, though they are too polite to say so. That is likely why modern researchers are now happy to have computer screens that generate the most completely neutral and least conjugal-relation-related stimulus conceivable: random dots; a flurry of random blips with no reason, rhyme, nor structure. The most common things people say they see in the completely random dots are faces. Science historian and writer Michael Shermer coined the term 'patternicity' for the relentless human tendency to find significant patterns amidst random things. He explains that the brain is by nature a meaning-making dot-connector, because there is greater benefit in seeing patterns and meaning where there are none, than there are potential pitfalls in failing to identify things in the world that might nourish or threaten us. Our very constitution compels us to discern objects (and create narratives) even when there is no thing out there, nor any genuine connection between random events. The mind is designed to err on the side of seeing connections, no matter how embarrassing.

In the words of a famous artist, ". . .if you look at any walls spotted with various stains or with a mixture of different kinds of stones . . . you will be able to see in it a resemblance to various different landscapes adorned with mountains, rivers, rocks, trees, plains, wide valleys, and various groups of hills. You will also be able to see diverse combats and figures in quick movement, and strange expressions of faces, and outlandish costumes, and an infinite number of things ... as with the sound of bells, in whose clanging you may discover every name and word that you can imagine." Leonardo Da Vinci – from *Percepts on Painting*, published posthumously in 1540.

D: Dreams   Many things appear in dreams, and they can be very detailed and vivid. The things that appear in dreams are convincingly real, and can include hallways with many doors, leading on to a never-ending succession of rooms, each one containing as many things as anyone could ever imagine, and imagining is very much what you are doing. Unlike movies, where set designers and CGI graphic designers need top modeling and rendering skills to contrive engrossing scenes, your imagination has no trouble filling the mind's eye with overwhelming all-encompassing detail. Overwhelm is par for the course in dreams, sometimes leading up (just like in movies) to the climactic chase scene. It is never someone else being chased—it is always you. Unlike watching a movie, where the action happens to a hired actor and you follow along from the comfort of a lounge chair with cup holders, the action in dreams happens to you. Dreams are exclusively, and some might feel excessively focused on you, with a virtual bombardment of tensions, surprises, confrontations, morphing apparitions, and action that needs to be taken, all of it riveting your attention, and inescapable. This can get annoying. During the day, if things get too intense, it's nice to sit back, kick the feet up, listen to the radio, read Calvin & Hobbes, do a Sudoku, or have a cocktail. This never happens in dreams. And it seems a little unfair. When awake you can daydream—daydream about anything you want—pleasant things, challenges to overcome, people you'd like to ask over. At night, when asleep, you are rarely given that option. Instead, you are pretty much stuck with the mood, the challenges, the scenery, and the people that show up uninvited. Again: a bit unfair.

Oliver Sacks stated that the waking state was also like being in a dream, but a dream sculpted by the realities surrounding us. At night, however, these realities are put to bed, and no longer provide structure. Without reality constraints, any and all permutations and combinations of our warehouses of mental imagery are possible, and unconscious processes that hide in the background during wakefulness can take on roles in the theater of the mind, none of whom are hidebound to a script. Our senses still perceive things in the sleeping environment, like thunder, or what is playing on the radio, but when dreaming the mind will wildly morph and blend those sensory snippets with whatever else pops up on the stage.

Two constants: (1) things appear to progress in the form of a narrative (even if it is a wacky narrative, like a story made up by a four-year-old); and, (2) that you are the protagonist. Even in the light of meaninglessness, the mind insists on meaning. Even in the face of a spinning tombola of events, the mind experiences strings of disassociated things as an ongoing narrative, a story being told—all happening to the self that is the constant hub of experience both when dreaming and when awake. Though when awake, there are rules. And the things are more permanent. When awake it's also possible to passively watch others in public squares, in books, or on video screens and become more absorbed by their experiences than one's own—and to guide the imagination on its meanderings, and to choose to be absorbed in awe by the beauty of things in the world for as long as one wants. What dreams, in their chaos, illustrate most potently, is that we have a self that is the experiencer of experiences, and that this self inhabits a narrative. During the day we have the luxury to forget this.

D: Ducks, fake   "When I see a bird that walks like a duck and swims like a duck and quacks like a duck, I call that bird a duck." – Indiana poet James Whitcomb Riley (1849 – 1916). The earliest known duck decoys were discovered in excavation of the Lovelock Cave in Churchill County, Nevada in 1924. The flock of eleven fake ducks were made from string-tied tule, a grassy herb, and adorned with paint and feathers. Analysis of two samples using Accelerator Mass Spectrometry found that the fake ducks dated back to 130 B.C. and 300 B.C. The decoy ducks gave actual ducks the idea that the grasses painted and decorated with feathers had the skinny on an optimal roosting area, whereas the area was actually sub-optimal for roosting, as local Native Americans were waiting nearby with bows, nets, and traps. Similar to Hoosier poet James Whitcomb Riley's deducktive reasoning, real ducks on high identified the decoys as ducks because they had roughly duck-like form and appeared to be swimming like ducks: bobbing up and down in wavy water as ducks are wont to do. The real key to fooling real ducks was the undulating action that suggested motion of a duck paddling or relaxing, though a proper set of decoys today will also include the sleeping decoy (head tucked back over the shoulder) and the feeding decoy (head in the water; tail in the air). Maintenance of decoy ducks is essential as savvy ducks will recognize signs of wear and tear, or leaks, and will not be fooled by a leaky decoy. Individually carved decoys have an advantage over mass-produced industrial decoys, as real ducks can habituate to generic McDucks. It is not only the unique shape of the individually-fashioned decoy that makes them seem more authentic to real ducks, it is also the differences in weighting that makes each artisanal duck float in the water accentedly. Duck quacks can then be spoofed by the hunter, using a Duck Commander Camo Max or similar, with individual flair. Modern advances in fake duck technology include mechanical spinning wings—particularly useful when the water is calm—and decoys motorized to dip into the water as if having found food. The additional motion also directs the attention of real ducks toward the animated decoys and away from the nearby Labrador Retriever.

E: Egrets Egrets are white birds with thin black legs, long necks, and extended flat yellow bills (orange when breeding) often seen standing on one leg in the shallow water of ponds or marshland looking for fish or frogs. They are in the heron family, though smaller than the typical heron. They primarily wade to hunt, though can swim. They fly slowly, using only two wing flaps per second, and when in flight the neck is pulled back to form an 'S' shape. Egrets make nests of twigs in leaves in tall marsh rushes, or high up in trees. They are usually silent but do call to others with low croaking sounds.

F: Food The German language has over 100 words for snow ('Schnee'), including such beauties as 'schneeflockengleich' (soft and delicate as snow) and 'schneevergnüglich' (happy as snow). In German, as with the Eskimoan langauges, suffixes can be added to the base word to make more snow words. This kind of linguistic accordion-playing is not done in the English language, which is why there is only one word for snow (Thesaurus.com lists no synonyms, though potential candidates include 'powder', 'snowflake', and 'cocaine'). Still, in English, happily, we can add adjectives to create a blizzard of modified snow expressions (e.g., 'Wisconsin snow'; 'yellow snow'). In this sense, there are at least as many variations on 'snow' in English as in Eskimoan langauges, though in English there is a space in the middle. There are also innumerable English language words for food, but that is in no small measure because there are hundreds of thousands of species of edible plant (which, nicely, can be paired with the over 70,000 wines in production). Though the German language is still ahead in the single-word food number department since by making soup out of edible plants the number of food words instantly doubles (e.g., soup made of parsley root 'Petersilienwurzel' becomes 'Petersilienwurzelsuppe'), and triples if you use the leftover soup in a casserole ('Petersilienwurzelsuppenauflauf').

Not to be outdone, the English language menu has assembled an army of adjectives to beat the Germans, who do not stand a chance against the likes of 'Potée of Crisp but Tender Root of Hamburg Parsley, Hand-Plucked from the Verdant Pastoral

Pastureland of Vermont, en Casserole'. To tip a chapeau toward the Europeans, menus originated in France in the 1770s. Prior to that there was no point to menus: eateries and take-aways peppered ancient Rome, since most common people spent their entire day out on the streets, tenement life being austere, but the ubiquitous 'thermapolia' did not need menus, with jars in masonry counters lining the street and displays plain to see just behind; in Medieval times the sole public eateries were roadside inns for travelers usually serving bread, cheese and a communal stew—locals did not eat there given the standards of both cuisine and hygiene, but they did imbibe there. Restaurants as places of leisure, along with menus, and individual tables instead of one common trough, developed in Paris in the late 1700s when it became a 'fashion' to be seen being served something special in public places. Visiting Britons would be surprised to see families supping together in restaurants, assuming that they were unable to feed themselves at home.

The early menus were written chalk on boards or recited by the waiter, while written menus, permitting more intimate perusal and reflection became the norm into the 1800s. Fast-forwarding to 1850, the printed menu at New York city's New York Hotel contained 40 items, only one of them expressed as a single word: 'Muffins'. 31 items consisted of two words (e.g., Sweet Omelette, Cold Lamb; Fried Liver) with the other 8 using three words (e.g., Boston Brown Bread; Salt Codfish, hashed). The closest thing to a vegetable was hominy boiled or fried, or potatoes boiled or stewed. There was no 'Cheekily Curvaceous Filet of Hand-Netted Cold-Water Long-Island-Sound Black Sea Bass, Gently Spanked until Tender then Flash-Sizzled in Panko Breadcrumbs till Golden Brown', as panko breadcrumbs were not invented until World War II when Japanese soldiers used electric current from tank batteries to cook what then became a crust-less bread, so as not to trigger thermal sensors on the battlefield. Instead, there was only 'Fresh Fish, Fried' on the 1850 New York Hotel menu.

This spartan approach to lists of food was typical of the time, but lacked the appeal to the imagination that would revolutionize the menu, and the idea of food. A few years later the menu of the Convention Supper of the 13th Anniversary of the Delta Kappa Epsilon Fraternity in Brunswick, Maine on August 5th, 1858 began to juice the salivary glands with such word salad embellishments as 'Sweet Bread, Larded, with Tomato Sauce', 'Boiled Capon, German Sauce', and 'Eels, Breaded with Ravigotte Sauce'. Early evidence of how menu words can be a dynamic factor in the idea of a dish, magnifying the pleasure in the meal, can be found on the 45-item 1854 menu of New York City's Astor House, which included 'Bastion of Goose Liver, with Truffles, on Pedestal', 'Cotelettes of Pigeon, Sauce Mareshale', 'Nougat of Flowers', and 'Ladies Fingers'. The evolution of the potency of menu description, which eventually became central to the idea of the meal, ultimately led to a time when if the kitchen ran out of pigeon, and quietly substituted chicken, the diner might be duped, but could still be enthralled by the meal, due to the menu magic conjured by the word 'cotelettes'.

Fast forward to the Los Angeles area in 2012, where a customer entered a sandwich shop to order a vegetarian sandwich listed on the menu as having alfalfa sprouts. After finding no alfalfa sprouts in the sandwich, the pursuant class action lawsuit resulted in an out-of-court settlement, permitting anyone who had purchased that sandwich to apply for a voucher good for a side order of soda, chips, cookie or pickle. The false representation of alfalfa sprouts in the sandwich was illegal in Los Angeles, due to the local Truth in Menu law, which represented a threat to faux gently-spanked black sea bass throughout tinseltown.

'Menu engineering' is a field of study that blends psychology and marketing, and includes both the placement of item within menus (e.g., special box with larger type for the most profitable items) and wording ('a la mode' vs. 'scoop of ice cream'), though restaurateurs have long been aware that certain terms, like 'mama's own', and particularly the vital adjective 'fresh', contributed more to the idea of a meal than the dubiously-sourced ingredients themselves. Some were also aware that diners were not watching when the delivery truck unloaded that morning, or last week. Or the week before. Jan Whitaker, in her remarkable 'Restaurant-ing Through History' blog, traces the truth-in-menu movement to Fisherman's Wharf in San Francisco in the 1970s, where 'fresh local' fish was often brought in frozen from afar, and other chef masterpieces were often reheated packaged units brought in frozen from the trucks—something common around the country, noting how a Chicago food writer in 1974 said it was futile to discuss which restaurant had the best lasagna, as they all tended to have been trucked in from the same handful of factories. Jan Whitaker details the margarine for butter, Maine lobster from who-knows-where, assembled & glued filet mignon, and the abuse of menu adjectives that led to a spate of truth-in-menu laws that were, bitterly, hard to enforce.

Fresh squeezed orange juice? Yes: freshly squeezed when it came off the tree in Florida, not in the restaurant. Scallops? Or cookie-cuttered shark meat. Vermont maple syrup? Or high fructose corn syrup with added flavor designed by computers. Truffle oil? Or adventures in modern chemistry. Multiple different fish offerings on the menu, each one more expensive than the next? Or fines handed down to a Malibu restaurant when they were found to all be the same fish.

Despite the truth-in-menu ordinance enacted in Los Angeles in 1973, not only might a veggie sandwich sometimes be short some sprouts, but DNA analysis of fish from groceries, restaurants, and sushi spots by Oceana found that a full 52% of fish tested in Southern California were not as advertised. Their findings reported in 2013 found that of 120 'red snapper' tested across the United States, only 7 (yes, seven) were actually red snapper. Of 241 sushi samples from 118 different sushi spots only a meager 24% of samples were the fish they claimed (including zero of the 23 yellowtail sushi actually being yellowtail). Still, the idea of red snapper—so colorful. So happy-snappy.

F: Fumbyx Small but vicious woodland mammal that looks more like a cross between a sea anemone and a lychee nut due its spools of dreadlockily-knotted fur, but with jagged, razor-like teeth. Fumbii hide in hollows, like wooden boxes, while readying themselves for savage and merciless attack.

F: Fuzzy Logic Fuzzy logic does not refer to how fuzzy creatures like dogs, cats and fumbii apply reasoning abilities to learning and problem-solving situations as one might think it would, although one essential aspect of feline learning does begin to help explain their seemingly random, mercurial, and impossible nature. If cat #1 has learned to open a door by leaping at the door handle, so that it unlatches the lock momentarily and the momentum of the leaping cat opens the door, cat #2, waiting by the door, and wanting to get out, will not attempt the same leap. Cat #2, when wanting to get out, will wait by the door hoping that either: a) the human of the house open it; b) cat #1 will leap at the door handle to open the door; or, c) the door will magically open on its own [see Magic]. Although cat #2 has seen cat #1 opening the door by leaping at the handle multiple times—perhaps its entire life—cat #2 will not learn how to open the door that way, unless some time in the future it jumps off the kitchen counter and inadvertently hits the door handle, opening the door in the process. The memory of the event will then be in cat #2's repertoire, and it will have learned how to open the door. But it cannot learn by watching another cat doing the same.

Humans, on the other hand, do indeed learn by watching others—even by watching cats. By watching cats, we can learn when the tin roof is hot. Humans then can apply tin roof heat knowledge to other situations, like assuming the car roof is also hot, so as not to set the cat down on it while opening the car door on the way to the vet which, for the cat, is worse than a hot tin roof.

Not only do we learn by imagining analogy, our brains also model what others do. When child #1 plays with a ball in class, although it is not permitted, child #2 watching the play will have parallel neurons activated in the motor cortex—the same brain region involved in ball-playing, not just the one involved in watching. This contributes to unauthorized behaviors in classrooms 'going viral', constrained only by the number of children in the classroom who remain in the thrall of the hypnotist behind the desk.

Not only will toddlers open a door by depressing the handle when they observe a cat doing so, they will skip the leap entirely most of the time. A toddler will then apply the idea of 'opening door by monkeying around with door protrusion' to any and all possible doors, which adults might call 'getting into mischief', but which is really the dynamic expression of the cognitive adaptation of generalizing knowledge and extrapolating it to analogous situations, using fuzzy logic. They will use the observation of the cat on a levered door and attempt to apply it to doors with knobs, doors with latches, and even the big door knockers with huge iron loops like on the portals of ancient cathedrals. This cognitive flexibility will serve them all their lives until they arrive at an Airbnb in Holland and find a door that will not unlock until you first lift the handle into the up position, whereupon they will use their flexible cognition to contact the Airbnb host on the mobile phone.

Fuzzy logic is at the heart of human thinking and is essential because ideas are squishy. Computers have had to employ binary logic, classically exemplified in the pocket calculator, which is neither squishy nor fuzzy. Attempts are made in the field of Artificial Intelligence to program computers with fuzzy logic, but to do so, an algorithm needs to be designed that finds vague, sifty-sorty, amorphous similarities between things, and the problem then becomes that algorithms are themselves not fuzzy either.

Fuzzy logic then explains why we dress dogs up in cute outfits. It makes vague sense that Scottie thinks the kilt looks cute, and will feel a certain pride in bravehearted clannish heritage. It just feels right—though not for the pooch.. Fuzzy logic of the anthropomorphic sort, applied to furry creatures, as with most doggie clothing, isn't always a good fit. Alexandra Horowitz, who, in addition to talking illuminating walks with experts, heads the Dog Cognition Lab at Columbia University's Barnard College, reports, among her many insights, that when a dog looks guilty, it is not guilty, it is instead anticipating, or experiencing, punishment. We use fuzzy logic to project how we ourselves would feel if we chewed up the newspaper before anyone else could read it and were confronted with the evidence. And truth be told, it is exceedingly unlikely that Skippy really appreciates that great big conciliatory hug.

As clothing goes, dogs don't want things on their bodies—worst of all the vision-addling sunglasses, even if they go perfectly with Skippy's bikini. As fuzzy logic with furry friends goes, sometimes you're better off taking the Lab to a lab. Still, if you have a symbiotic relationship with your pet, then it is a symbiotic relationship with your pet—live it, enjoy it. Who's to say: maybe in the future dogs will determine canine social hierarchy based upon their attire as humans do now—Scotties flaunting their lineage in tartans and kilts—with painfully ill-fittingly garmentry becoming as essential in the puppy pecking order as status-cementing corsetry was in the French royal court of the 1500s.

G: Games Games are things that help people, young and old, simulate the important decisions and actions required in real life situations, but using play money. A dolly lets young humans grease the yet-dormant gears of parenthood. Legos teach construction skills and how minefields work. The board game Chutes and Ladders helps develop skills for coping with devastating setbacks. The board game Monopoly hones skills for becoming stinking rich or pi$$ poor. Parcheesi, Ludo, Trouble and Sorry! are not the names of understandably miserable dwarves, but are essentially the same game, which develops understanding of man's inhumanity to man, along with social skills related to revenge and vindictiveness. Pin The Tail On The Donkey develops spatial awareness despite inadequate visual input, such in the case of a sudden power outage, in the face of ongoing ridicule. Bumper Saucers teach what not to do when piloting a real vehicle. Scrabble provides an initiation into the arcane pantheon of two-letter words, and sometimes four.

G: **Gander, proper**   [see: Gaslighting]

G: **Gaslighting**   The political equivalent of getting people to bawk like a chicken [or proper gander].

G: **Giant Stone Balls of Costa Rica**   The giant stone balls of Costa Rica were discovered in the 1930s by workers from the United Fruit Company who were clearing jungle for banana plantations—bananas which are now long departed from this earth, though the giant stone balls remain. The over 300 balls are almost perfectly round, and in sizes ranging from fist-sized to 8.7 feet in diameter. Most were found to have been made from gabbro, a form of basalt, shaped by hammering against other rocks then smoothing with sand. They became a national symbol of Costa Rica, are exhibited in Costa Rican government buildings, and have inspired other (round) art. [See: Y]

H: Hawthorns   "Oh, my poor little hawthorns," I was assuring them through my sobs, "it is not you that want to make me unhappy, to force me to leave you. You, you have never done me harm. So I shall always love you." And, drying my eyes, I promised them that, when I grew up, I would never copy the foolish example of others, but that even in Paris, on fine spring days, instead of paying calls and listening to silly talk, I would make excursions into the country to see the first hawthorn-trees in bloom." – Marcel Proust from *Swann's Way*

I: Imagination   [entry currently unavailable due to ongoing remodeling]

J: Jump to Letter K

K: Kaleidoscope   A thing that makes things kaleidoscopic.

L: Lamb   Little lamb, who made thee? Dost thou know who made thee? Gave thee life, and bid thee feed—by the stream and o'er the mead; gave thee clothing of delight—softest clothing, woolly, bright; gave thee such a tender voice, making all the vales rejoice? Little lamb, who made thee? Dost thou know who made thee? Little lamb, I'll tell thee. Little lamb, I'll tell thee: He is called by thy name, for He calls Himself a Lamb. He is meek, and he is mild, he became a little child. I a child, and thou a lamb, we are called by His name. Little lamb, God bless thee! Little lamb, God bless thee! – William Blake, from *Songs of Innocence* 1789

L: Liposuction   [fatuous entry removed]

M: Magic   Magic is manipulation of attention, like stage magician Harry Blackstone, with his donkey tricks. Blackstone would pull silk scarves out of not-so-thin air until there was a huge pile of scarves on the floor. Then he would reach into the pile of scarves and pull out a live donkey. Even people who saw him perform the trick multiple times couldn't figure out how he did it. That was because at the very moment when ladies wearing lustrous wings and very little else suddenly cavorted across the stage, Blackstone would go behind the curtain and calmly bring out the donkey. He performed a similar trick with a top hat on the stage that he covered with a large cloth, before starting to hand items to his lovely assistant. No one would notice a second, less-fetching assistant calmly walking the donkey onto the stage, although it was happening in plain view. He would then remove the cloth from the top hat, and it would be on the head of the donkey. It was actually a burro—a small type of donkey not much bigger than a dog, but it is the idea of a donkey that mattered to the public.

It is common to think that there are two kinds of magic: 1) stage magic with card tricks, donkeys, rabbits-out-of-hats, and failing to saw a person in half; versus, 2) real magic, which typically involves incantations & spells, psychic surgery, brewing large quantities of newts in cauldrons, bending spoons, and the ever-popular voodoo. Both types of magic are manipulation of attention. Manipulation of attention is also used in teaching (you; seat; teacher); cinema (you; seat; screen); and pickpocketing (you; mustard on jacket; helpful stranger).

M: Mixer Settings The brain does not think like a computer, but it does synthesize inputs like a multi-channel studio mixing console. Just like a studio mixer, it inputs different signals from the environment (e.g., snare drum, vocals, tambourine, the cat), then modulates each one by pushing channel faders low, high, or all the way off, to sculpt the most satisfying mix. Channel faders are amped up or ramped down to tone down brassiness in the brass, to soften kick drum kick, and to let the right voices be heard, making life a dynamic mix of new tunes and familiar oldies, dappled by rockin' and rappin', psychobilly and trance—a symphony with the ultimate goal of making each day a #1 hit. To the extent the brain is like a multi-channel studio mixing console, *the faders getting the most amping up and ramping down action over the course of the day seem to be:*

Wakefulness/Alertness – The mixer console 'on/off' button. When off, there is deep sleep or coma. When on, there is some degree of alertness. The reticular activating system in the brain stem determines when the body sleeps and wakes, and no-one knows exactly why or when.

Arousal – When first waking up this fader is hardly engaged (gradual notching up from 0 to 1). Rolling out of bed ups the fader another notch (2). Bracing cleansing and teeth brushing brings moments of lucidity (3-4). Depending on the amount of coffee then imbibed, the fader can take a big jump (5-7) and may spike suddenly when realizing you're going to miss the bus (9). Other fader-poppers are doorbells, ringing phones, barking dogs, and politics. Later, when it is 5'clock somewhere, the arousal fader can mellow happily out.

Internal Monologue – Some people feel they are constantly speaking to themselves over the course of the day, 'hearing' their own virtual voice in their heads, while some report never hearing an inner monologue narrative. Most have it going some of the time and not others (like auto-faders that will move on their own). Others report they can amp it up or turn it off at will (active fader fiddling).

Attentive to Surroundings vs. Lost in Thought – You can look out the window and see things or look out the window and not even realize you are looking out the window. This fader tends to shift on its own over the course of the day as the situation warrants, though people naturally predisposed to 'absorption' will find themselves lost in thought more often. If the fader is engaged in 'attentive' mode, then a parallel fader can be employed to toggle between broad, general attention, versus narrow concentrated focus on one specific interest or task.

Anxiety – This fader can behave like a regular roller coaster over the course of the day; sometimes subtle (1-3), sometimes motivating (4-7), sometimes paralyzing (8-10).

Sensual vs. Cerebral – Why people go to the spa.

Taking Initiative vs. Going With the Flow – Making decisions to take action; choosing tacks to take; actively altering mood to be most beneficial; deciding to create ideas and things—versus letting things happen, or just doing what comes natural. This is a manually controlled fader.

Recording studios also add 'effects' to sounds. Different qualities of reverb can make it sound like the singer is standing in a tiled bathroom, the Cologne cathedral, or the Zhayangzong Cavern in Tibet. Effect filters add tone and texture to the original input, just as the mind adds feeling, tone and texture: making some things glowing & warm vs. others ominous; some things standing out vs. others blending into the background; some things meaningful & inspiring vs. hum of the drum. *The semi-opaque acetate overlays of the mind's effects faders can well include*:

Rose-Colored Glasses – A line of research finds that undue optimism—to the point of self-deception—is both normal for people, and likely useful. Going through the world happy and optimistic ignores certain unpleasant realities that more circumspect or depressed people may see more realistically, but rose-colored glasses appear healthier for self-esteem, motivation, coping with stress, and for positive social relations. There is also research to show that positive mood alters visual perception—increasing the range of stimuli the mind attends to—whereas low mood results in a narrower range of visual focus.

Dreaming in Black & White vs. Color – Since 1915 people have been asked about the color of their dreams. Into the 1950s respondents reported that dreams were predominantly in black and white (like most movies and television at the time); in a 1951 study 29% of dreams were reported to include some color, but by the 1960s 83% of reported dreams involved color. The work of psychologist Eva Murzyn of of the University of Edinburgh points to a possible critical period in childhood, when exposure to B&W or color media might influence how dreams appear throughout life. Confounding the issue is that no-one knows how the dream actually appeared when sleeping, because all reporting of dreams is done when awake. A person who has awoken may remember a dream, but is no longer experiencing the dream itself—they are experiencing the representation of a recollection of a dream. It is impossible to truly know if a color or B&W filter is applied until one is awake, to whatever chimerical memory of the dream is retrievable—or to what extent the recollection of the dream at all matches what happened when asleep.

The Sacred vs. The Profane – Romanian historian and philosopher of religion Mircea Eliade lamented that humanity was moving from living a sacred experience, within a sacred sphere, into a biological/economic era. He saw living with a sacred frame on the world as being a different mode of being, and having a different order of reality, than the plain, perfunctory profane frame, and gave the example of a stone. In the profane view a stone is a stone like any other, with no properties other than its shape and hardness, but for those for whom a stone is seen as sacred, that stone is metamorphosed into having a supernatural reality. Medieval cathedrals each had their sacred relics—bones of saints or Shroud of Turin. These specific relics were viewed as sacred apart from the mundane world surrounding them, but Eliade also describes all of the world as having sacred dimensions to a person living in that mode: sacred space, sacred time, and being at the center of the world. This experiencing of all the world as sacred was expressed by Benedictine abbess Hildegard of Bingen (1098-1179); "Everything that is in the heavens, on earth, and under the earth is penetrated with connectedness, penetrated with relatedness"; "All living creatures are sparks from the radiation of God's brilliance, emerging from God like the rays of the sun"; and, as things go, "There is the music of Heaven in all things." Given the continuing ubiquity of religious practice and experience worldwide, it is likely that this fader is, despite any gentle nudging of the general tendency toward the profane, still very much in active use, though each region and each individual may have it engaged to varying degree. And even for those who might imagine it is no more operable, or has lost all input signal, Eliade warns that those who feel themselves totally secular, and living in a desacralized world, should be aware that they are actually still subject to an active influence. The channel is still fully functional; the full effect repertoire is still actively coloring experience, and if they are not paying attention, they may find themselves amping full bore into faux religion, and twisted myth.

Some fader configurations are fairly fixed. Some people (a) have 'perfect pitch'—if they are sitting at the DMV and hear a 'bing' to announce the next customer, they can tell you it is A-flat. Most people (b) can't name that note, but they can tell you if someone singing is in tune or not. Then there are those lucky people, (c) who never experience anyone's singing as out of tune, and these are the fans of Florence Foster Jenkins who are not laughing. People (c) who have no idea of pitch cannot imagine that there are people (b) who laugh when they hear Florence Foster Jenkins, but those same people with typical sense of pitch (b) would never imagine that there are (a) people with perfect pitch unless they prove it by identifying random tones. People in groups (a), (b), and (c) have their faders fixed within a certain range, and it is impossible for them to know that there are other people who don't experience pitch the same way, unless they all listen to Florence Foster Jenkins at the same time and compare 'notes'.

We tend to assume that others have the same basic inputs as ours, though some might only hear the drums, some might experience a pervasive 100 Hz hum on some signals; some might not have particular input cables connected at all. Likewise, we tend to assume that others have similar fader range and variability as we do—though a fader of theirs might be fixed at a setting different than ours, or push into a range that we can't reach. It is impossible to conceive of such a setting or range, because ours never goes there. Some may have, say, emotional reactivity always operating within the low end of the range (cool mellow), or high end (big intensity) and some may find the fader even trending into the red zone (freak out), a level at which the input signal gets busted up completely, like the fuzz or shred of distortion on an electric guitar, or choppy/squealy digital 'clipping'. As Neuroscientist David Eagleman tells in Incognito, we have little understanding—nor can we have the understanding—of what someone else's brain perceives. Each brain operates with different input filters and different processing parameters, and the experience of reality (and the resulting song) rendered by each person's configurations will be unique to each individual. *Some of the more inscrutable or perhaps even unfathomable operational settings might include:*

Channels That Overlap – In most people audio input is experienced as softer or louder on the sound channel, and visual input plays on the vision channel, but about 4% of people have seemingly unrelated fader channels that move in synchrony. Those who experience synesthesia might smell a particular smell when they hear a certain sound, or see different colors when they engage people with different personalities ('auras'). There are at least 50 mixed synesthesia modalities, which act like faders latched together on a studio mixer; two-thirds of synesthetes share the most common pairing: seeing every letter on the printed page as having its own color. These colors are not the same for all synesthetes, although the letter 'A' tends toward red for many, but in any case a black & white printed newspaper will be Technicolor for about 2% of all of the people you meet. For some the effect is subtle, for others vivid, but brain scans show that increased white-matter connections in sensory areas of synesthetes activate more than one sensory region at a time. One synesthete musician describes seeing colors that match the musical notes and chords she is playing—appearing both as a general wash of color, at the edges of her field of vision. but also as dotted accents of other colors, when specific notes play over a chord; what's more, she describes physical sensations on her skin in response to the tone of passages, from silky, to warm, to hugging to stabbing. Some of the most delicious descriptions of synesthesia come from James Wannerton, who experiences complex and diverse tastes for the sounds of words, and has detailed the tastes of every station on the London Tube, his favorite being Tottenham (sausage) Court (crispy egg) Road (toast), a station that makes for a complete breakfast. Depending on the Tube station name, the taste can fade quickly or last for an extended period of time, and will activate stomach acids. His specific flavor associations have been consistent since childhood (e.g., one grandmother's name has always tasted of condensed milk), indicating to researchers that these are genuine physical responses, and not simply the result of the fader of imagination amped up into the red zone. Although this hard-wiring appears to be a genetic trait common to a small percentage of individuals, almost half of all people will experience synesthesia after just 5 minutes in a sensory deprivation tank.

Seeing Forest vs. Seeing Trees – Tudor scholar John Heywood's *A Dialogue Conteinyng the Nomber in Effect of all the Prouerbes in the Englishe Tongue*, published in 1546, includes a proverb concerning a person who, "can not see the wood for trees." The centuries-long endurance of this trope (now often expressed as, 'can't see the forest for the trees') might relate to the fact that the right cerebral hemisphere of the brain has faculties that conceive of things globally as wholes (forest) while the left cerebral hemisphere includes faculties with more linear, detailed, step-by-step analytical functions (ideal for seeing individual trees). Both are vital: when retreating from King Henry's longbowers at the Battle of Agincourt fleeing French infantry would have needed to shift perspective between the general idea of a forest to flee toward, as well as the individual trees to shelter behind. Similarly, scientists in the lab need to shift perspective between the broad goal of an experiment (forest) as well as what is overflowing from specific test tubes (trees). Flexible forest/tree fader flopping is essential for functioning, but subject to individual differences, vividly seen in the case of autism. Cognitive scientist Uta Frith (wife of Chris) has found that a common feature in autism is strong focus on detail (or minutiae, or only the light fixtures at cocktail parties), to the point of ignoring broader context, or 'context blindness'. Neurological differences have been documented to match in autistic subjects, including a large number of unintegrated short-distance connections in the pre-frontal cortex, and fewer long-range connections that would allow shifting of attention from minutiae to global contexts. There are, however, benefits: the difference thus permits intense concentration on things of interest, which can lead to excellence in developed areas of expertise.

Dot Connecting – For those with the random-dot-connecting 'patternicity' fader near zero, a smattering of random dots is just that. For those with the fader set higher the dots appear to form patterns: things like a dipping pot with a handle, a big bear & a little bear, a hunter with a sword on the belt, a crab, a lion, and twins named Gemini. For those with the 'patternicity' fader cranked up to the max the dots are clearly an alien spaceship sent here to take over the world. Higher fader settings have been linked to higher levels of the neurotransmitter dopamine in brain systems.

Self-Identity Signal Strength – Ranges from dissociative fugue state (losing all awareness of who one is sometimes followed by traveling cross country and not remembering how one got there (fader disengaged) to viewing oneself the way the Catholic Church viewed planet earth before Copernicus. Low settings are associated with living in the moment, having interest in what is happening in the surroundings, and interest in the experience and perspective of others. Very high settings are known to fill the mind with thoughts related to one's personal triumphs, perceived wrongs done to one by others, concatenations of personal anecdotes, and how normally trivial events affect number-one and why this is important.

Baseball Shortstops vs. People Who Miss Their Subway Stop – American psychologist Auke Tellegen created the Tellegen Absorption Scale to measure individual differences in how captivated or immersed people become in their experiences and imagination. Baseball shortstops are very alert. They have no time to daydream. They cannot afford to have their interest tweaked by the vintage design twist on the uniform of the opposing batter, or to have the stadium organ music transport them back to ballparks of their youth, lest they become distracted and miss the line drive headed straight for their cranium. Baseball shortstops need their absorption faders set near nil, whereas those who score high in absorption are off galavanting their way through romance novels, reliving intrepid life adventures, and experiencing altered states of consciousness. Engrossed by melodrama, pampered by the breezes of the subway doors opening and closing, and swept away by the station platform Muzak, those with high absorption fader levels can soar to places where fantasy comes alive, where time stands still, and where they miss their stop.

Sensitivity – Some individuals appear to have stronger physiological or emotional responses to sensory stimuli, as well as to mind-provoking ideas than others. Strong reactions to sound, or bright lights, or tags on clothing is common in autism, but variations in reactivity to what the senses perceive are wide ranging—and are by nature unique to each individual, in ways that others cannot really know. Some may have a strong and quick response to emotion-provoking stimuli or ideas (going from 0 to 60 in a flash); or may have a high threshold before emotional triggers have effect (calm even in a crisis). Some might be overcome with awe and passion in the face of natural wonders while others just get out the camera. No matter how elaborately those with heightened sensitivities try to explain what is happening to them to others, the response they get is often, "Uh-huh, that's nice"—because others naturally frame what they are hearing in terms of their own set parameters, because that is all they can truly know. Our own pattern of sensitivities becomes the default framework for trying to comprehend what other people are feeling, no matter what words they use or how impassioned they get.

Wagner's 'Ring of the Nibelungen' vs. 'Chopsticks' – Although both musical works were completed in the 1870s, the former has a playing time over 15 hours, involves Valkyries & funeral pyres, was written for a huge orchestra with extra brass and needed its own theater built to perform it, while the latter is sometimes played by kindergartners using two fingers. Wagner was also known for stage settings with fire-rimmed mountaintops, steam machines, lightning and mechanical dragons—conjuring a visual spectacle to match the epic grandeur of the Ring. Similarly, there are some people who can instantly conjure an entire Wagnerian theater set in their minds with the slightest suggestion, versus those who need buy a ticket for the theater. The first exploration into individual differences in mental imagery was initiated by scientist Francis Galton in 1880, who wrote, "I desire to define the different degrees of vividness with which different persons have the faculty of recalling familiar scenes under the form of mental pictures, and the peculiarities of the mental visions of different persons." Although his finding that scientists have 'feeble' mental imagery has since been challenged, research in 2020 by Cognitive scientist Alan Zeman of the University of Exeter did find that a significant number of people with 'aphantasia' (the inability to see mental imagery) chose careers in the sciences, while a high number of people with 'hyperphantasia' (prone to producing exceptionally vivid mental imagery) chose careers in creative pursuits like arts and design. The ~2% of people with very limited visualization abilities still comprehend descriptions and stories they hear, but don't use pictures in the mind to conceive of them, whereas with hyperphantasia (which is more common than aphantasia) hearing a story being told will create an image as clear and precise in the mind as if a play were being performed right there on the spot. Mental images for hyperphantasiacs are so rich and detailed that it can become difficult to differentiate between what is real or what the imagination conjures up. And hearing or reading descriptions of pain, or beauty, can evoke strong physical responses. Hyperphantasia has similarities to 'fantasy prone personality', described by psychologists Sheryl Wilson and Theodore Barber as found in individuals who may spend half their time daydreaming or fantasizing, have physiological reactions to things they imagine, can confuse fantasy with actual events, and in childhood might have had very convincing imaginary friends, or dolls and stuffed animals they considered living beings. Wilson & Barber estimated fantasy prone personality as happening for ~4% of people.

Clean Signal vs. Red Zone Distortion – One standard of quality in audio recording is 'signal to noise ratio'. 'Signal' refers to the sound of the singer or instrument. 'Noise' refers to hiss, buzz, crackle or hum (unless the singer is hissing, buzzing, crackling or humming on purpose). In the human ear 'noise' might be ringing sounds like from tinnitus, or crackling from water in the ear. In the visual system, 'noise' might be floaters or cataracts in the eyes, or hallucinations. Hallucinations are equivalent to pushing the fader so high that the dials are in the 'red zone' of distortion or digital clipping—this signifies that sounds are happening not as produced by the band. Hallucinations involve experiencing things that aren't there, though the only way to know for sure it was a hallucination is to perform verification checks, like doing a double take, or picking up the phone that seemingly rang to see if someone is on it. Even if it proves to be a hallucination, it was still real, because you very much had it. If people in white coats come into the room, you can honestly report, "I just saw Napoleon riding by on a donkey," and because you just hallucinated it, this would be 100% true—and pretty normal at that, because 10% to 15% of perfectly healthy people naturally experience some form of hallucination at some time (across any of the five senses), and there are also times when dream states seem to bleed into wakefulness. But if the people in white coats then ask, "Is it Napoleon who just delivered your copy of Le Monde?", and there is no copy of Le Monde, and you reply, "Yes, and he fluffed my pillow too," then it is likely that you have not just hallucinated, which can happen to anyone, you are also delusional. On the other hand, if you say to the people in white coats, "Are you all crazy? Seeing Napoleon was probably a visual phantasm caused by excitation of phosphenes when I rubbed my eyes too hard!", the people in white coats will then be assured that you are not delusional and put a corresponding check mark in a box on their clipboards. Then, you might ask the people in white coats how they got into your home and what they are doing in your bedroom.

One Sandwich Short of a Picnic vs. Out To Lunch – Memory is fuzzy; sometimes Swiss cheesy. Ideas people have can be flexible or fixed, and the fidelity of ideas to things that are true can be a good match, or a house afire. Professor of Psychiatry Ronald W. Pies in Alternative facts: A psychiatrist's guide to twisted relationships to truth describes a wide range of memory and reality characteristics from his professional practice, and they constitute a real smorgas-mixing-board of alternative fact and fantasy. Misstatement of fact can range from a simple 'Freudian slip' to Petticoat Junction. Memory gaffes can range from misstating the number of attendees at an inauguration, to relating events that could not possibly have happened—and when faced with contrary evidence the response could be a flexible blush and correction, or rigid and inflexible insistence on things that are utterly impossible. A reading of Dr. Pie's descriptions suggests this possible hierarchy of fader notches: (1-2) simple ordinary gaffes that everyone experiences from time to time (e.g., telling the officer you had a V-8, when you actually had a Bloody Mary); (3-4) 'over-held' ideas that are contrary to what most people believe but are still plausible (e.g., there are alligators under the bed); (5) rigidity or inflexibility in holding beliefs despite solid evidence to the contrary (e.g., I am chicken; hear me bawk); (6) false memories (e.g., a memory researcher suggests that you once went to Disneyland, though you've never been, and then you brag about your exploits on the bumper saucers); (7) rigidly held beliefs about things that can't possibly have basis in physical reality (e.g., my Pet Rock laid an egg); (8) difficulty discerning what is real vs. unreal; inability to distinguish between truth and fiction (e.g., Star Trek conventions); (9) 'confabulation': inventing elaborate stories you insist just happened; can develop after brain trauma or stroke; (10) mad as a hatter. The problem is, that the higher up the ladder one goes, the more impossible it is to discern that one is high up the ladder.

M: Monkey   Stop. Just stop.

M: Movies   On July 24th, 1964 Andy Warhol pointed a stationary Auricon motion-picture camera (it looks like a black box with big Mickey Mouse ears holding the film) at the Empire State Building ten minutes before sundown. He pushed the 400 asa film to 1000 to make the recording look grainy, and filmed for 6 1/2 hours at 24 frames per second. The resulting movie, *Empire*, debuted in March, 1965 in Manhattan, but was projected at 16 frames per second, slower than actual time, so that it would run for 8 hours. After about 10 minutes, dozens left the City Hall Cinema theater to ask for their money back. *Empire* broke the record for longest movie ever, which was previously also held by Andy Warhol with his 5 hour 20 minute *Sleep*, showing a man sleeping. Nine theatergoers went to the premiere of *Sleep*, though two of them soon left.

It is likely that these two films were unappreciated because they were less interesting than what normally goes on in people's minds, even if they are just sitting out on the porch with a piña colada. What is going on in people's minds, according to Antonio Damasio in *The Feeling of What Happens*, does, however, have a close parallel in movies, though not necessarily Warhol movies. The theater of the mind, unlike the static image of a skyscraper, has a protagonist (one that does more than just lie unconscious) in the form of the self: the person who engages with things, frames things uniquely, strings events together into meaningful sequences (in cinema called a 'plot'), and when that protagonist habituates to any particular scene, it seeks out new avenues of stimulation; it juggles and splices different impressions and ideas, to make the ongoing cinematography, soundtrack, & story more alive, vivid, and satisfying. Something more Stanley Kubrick epic than Warhol, if not a veritable Cecil B. DeMille. The marquee product must be spliced and edited to keep it entertaining and worthwhile because the theater of the mind has a captive audience of one, and there is no asking for your money back. As with the images that flicker on a cinema screen, the mind has a circumscribed display space for the images, sounds, and actions it manages to hold in focus. Neuroscientist Christof Koch observes that in any waking moment, we simply don't experience all that many things at the same time. Attention has a limited theater of operations. And the same way that Hollywood directors select scenes and structure events to build a narrative, the mind also selects its experiences, orders its images, and interprets them with the help of a range of favorite story lines.

Enter Frederico Fellini. Felllini films tend to upend space, time, and characters in a whirlwind of impressions, symbols, and splintered story elements: everything the mind is striving, every waking moment, to avoid. The mind seeks to take an endless succession of momentary sensory data (flashes of light on the retina, sounds in the cochlea, rumblings in the belly, whiffs in the olfactory bulb) and forge from that a seamless whole, and a life story. And where parts are missing, the mind fills in the gaps. Cognitive neuroscientist Michael Gazzinaga reported in The Mind's Past that there is a story teller, a spin doctor, working in the left cerebral hemisphere, that spins narratives—not only providing continuity and cohesiveness to all that happens to us, but also cultivating and maintaining the story of ourselves. Donald Brown in *Human Universals* finds that all human cultures have the idea of one's self as separate from other selves, that each self has a private inner life, along with narrative, folklore, and myth. The primacy of narrative is illustrated in Oliver Sacks' observation that young children crave information in the form of stories, and learn best from narrative (not as much from encyclopedias or Warhol movies). The role of narrative is essential in our lives, as it is at the very crux of defining the self.

M: Museums   Museums are very, very large collections of things. The Smithsonian Institution has over 150 million things, and if it didn't there would be nothing to see there. Things in the Smithsonian are individually cataloged, which actually makes 300 million things: the thing itself, and the catalog entry. There is also a placard next to each thing exhibited with a description of the item (further thing inflation). The very fact of being in a museum adds a quality and value to a thing, making that particular thing more special than similar things that got sent to landfills or are still buried in Mesopotamia. Someday, the Smithsonian placards themselves are likely to be items of value worthy of exhibition in museums.

Unfortunately, some of the things in museums are not what placards say they are. Some of the things are fake. The Brooklyn Museum learned using the latest forensic techniques that about one quarter of the Friedsam Collection of paintings, porcelain, and precious artifacts donated in 1932 were fraudulent. In 2013 they had a choice: (1) continue to exhibit the fake items (though visitors might not be impressed); or, (2) get rid of them—but the contractual terms of the collection donation prohibited them from dumping only the fake ones while keeping the legit items; and storing the fakes would cost an initial $400,000 to have them put in storage, and then another $250,000 per year in maintenance costs. The forging of art and antiquities is as old as art and antiquities are. Forgeries themselves can become objects of interest, character, and value. In 2010 the Victoria & Albert Museum opened an exhibit featuring the work of Shaun Greenhalgh, whose forgeries of both ancient and modern art—from painting to sculpture to metalwork—created between 1989 and 2006, were purchased by museums for prices into the six-figure range. They were great forgeries, and the extensive range of Greenhalgh's artifice was an art of its own. Making the best of a bogus thing is also on display at the British Museum. When items from Baron Ferdinand Rothschild's 1898 Waddeston Bequest were found to be fakes they were kept on display with altered placards. The British Museum recognized their value in terms of classic fakery cultural history—as well as for their pure beauty, no matter how artfully devious the origin.

N: New Thought   At the turn of the century (not this one: the last one) a movement grew that championed the use of the imagination as a tool for self-betterment. In centuries prior, people had primarily relied on gods and spirits to take care of that for them, either through grace, or in exchange for a goat. Living in a sacred sphere, it could be blasphemy to promote the idea that it was up to your lonesome to chart the navigation of your own soul, with your own moral compass. The idea that you could alter your own thinking for health and well-being, instead of relying on chapters and verses to do the alterations for you, was condemned as heresy in 417 A.D. when British monk Pelagius was excommunicated by Pope Innocent I for asserting that people are born with freedom to choose for themselves what is good, instead of having God do it for them. But by 1893 New Thoughtist Henry Wood felt safe enough from torture and summary execution (not to mention eternal damnation) to write in his 1893 publication with a cool name *Ideal Suggestion through Mental Photography*: "The soul's real world is that which it has built of its thoughts, mental states, and imaginations." In a profane world, those thoughts could sometimes, um, wander. With mental states untethered, and the imagination unscriptured, New Thought taught that we ought not be distraught, or lost in odd thought, nor wait for providence to do what it wants, but as expressed by Horatio W. Dresser in 1899: "One is to learn to marshal the tendencies of the mind," for, "the attainment of self-control," to achieve desired goals.

The method for manifesting manna from heaven was not to go out stand in a pasture with a basket and wait, but to form and hold the mental image of falling manna, so as to actively attract manna to one's self. Horatio W. Dresser said, ". . . one's thought should be centered on the ideal outcome"; Henry Wood stressed that thinking, "be turned upon grand ideals until it forms a habit and creates a well-worn channel."

If this sounds like Norman Vincent Peale's 1952 *The Power of Positive Thinking*, and Wayne W. Dyer's 1978 *Pulling Your Own Strings*, and Rhonda Byrne's 2006 *The Secret*, that's because it is. It is mental magic. Magic is the direction of attention, and New Thought taught to think about what you want. If that is what you think about, that is what will be happening for you.

If you think positive thoughts, then positive thoughts are the ideas you will be having.

Modern day opportunity for workshops and training in thinking these kind of thoughts abound, and also permeate television advertisements. But if a weekend in Sedona proves too expensive, or if self-help books get mind-numbingly repetitive, a panoply of positive thoughts is in easy reach on the radio—with the added bonus that they will repeat themselves interminably as 'earworms.' A spin through the dial is a veritable jukebox of such New-Thought-styled mantras as: Murphy & Chesney's "Everything's Gonna Be Alright"; Gloria Gaynor's "I Will Survive"; Louis Armstong's "What A Wonderful World"; Shawn Mendez's "There's Nothing Holdin' Me Back"; The Bee Gees "Stayin' Alive"; Katrina and the Waves "Walking on Sunshine"; Journey's "Don't Stop Believin'", and the inimitable Monty Python's "Always Look On The Bright Side of Life". Some measure of caution is warranted (e.g., R. Kelly's "I Believe I Can Fly"), so it is recommended to choose an earworm responsibly. A realistic New Thought balance was struck by Roger Miller, country and novelty songwriter, winner of eleven Grammy awards, in his 1966 single that made it to #17 on the Billboard charts, "You Can't Rollerskate in a Buffalo Herd", where he notes that although fishing for yellowfin tuna in a watermelon patch will not yield yellowfin tuna no matter how single-focused and powerful the self control of the mind, you can still be happy if you exert mental effort toward being happy.

O: Orange   Orange you glad it ain't banana?

P: Peashooter   A tube like a bastardius, but far narrower. The peashooter has some of the properties of a turkey baster, but is not tapered at the end, and has no bulb at the other end, unless you consider human cheeks a form of bulb. If used to shoot darts instead of peas then it is by definition a blowgun, not a peashooter. If not used for shooting peas then it's just a tube like a bastardius, but far narrower.

P: People, other   There is ongoing debate about whether other people know us better than we know ourselves, or whether we know ourselves better than other people know us. Evidence for us knowing other people better than they know themselves is at its purest with first impressions, before people can start to use charms and wiles to convince you they are someone different. Anyone who works as a cashier sees an endless parade of people every day, and immediately determines who is outgoing or mopey or alert or quirky or scary or lost-looking or quick-responding or happy or sleepy or bashful or grumpy or dopey—all things that the ~~dwarfs~~ customers themselves seem to be unaware of. The customers all think that they are perfectly fine people, in complete control, while going about the business of making assumptions about the cashier. In *How The Mind Works* Steven Pinker observes that the human species has remarkable ability to draw information from others' facial expressions, along with great estimation of motives and attitudes from subtle nuance in others' words and behavior. This is not 'mind reading', this is the intuitive psychology that comes as factory standard equipment.

The case for people knowing themselves better than others know them centers on the fact that our thoughts and perceptions are ours alone and cannot be perceived by others, across so many levels and dimensions. Other people are most privy, attentive, and perceptive to those outward behaviors of ours that impact them. A pickpocket uses clothing cues to determine if a person is a tourist, gesture cues that indicate that the mark is more attentive to the Eiffel Tower than the wallet, and posture & movement cues to determine whether the mark is spry & vigilant vs. exhausted & jaded from sightseeing all day, before deciding who to spill mustard on. The pickpocket has no way of knowing whether the mark can read auras, believes the earth is flat, or is in a mid-life crisis, and the pickpocket doesn't care.

To compound the situation, according to William James, "Whenever two people meet, there are really six people present,", consisting of the two people as they see *themselves*, the two as they are seen by the other person, and each person as that person *really is*. William James ups the ante by adding, "A man has as many social selves as there are distinct groups of persons about whose opinion he cares. He generally shows a different side of himself to each of these different groups."

Not to be outdone in terms of complicating matters by a 19th Century psychologist, contemporary neuroscience reveals that when we are in the presence of others, we tend to absorb aspects of who they are, mirror their presentation, adopt some of their characteristics, and take a good soaking bath in their feelings and ideas. In *Making Up The Mind* Chris Frith notes that there is good reason aspects of others are contagious, and that we become like them: this unconscious blending allows us to understand others better, and predict their actions. According to Frith, our actions and our thought are shaped by people we engage with, even when we imagine that we are separate entities, walled off from others, encapsulated by bodies and minds all our own. The membranes of personality and mind are much more porous than the six people know.

P: Placebo   A placebo is the idea of doing or taking something to feel better when one is feeling ill (which can very well happen with a placebo)—or to imagine that a genuine physical malady or disease is remedied or cured (this does not actually happen with a placebo, if it is a quality placebo). The physical thing or action that becomes the idea of a placebo can be most anything: a pill, a ritual incantation done in full headdress, a kiss on the owie, a new car. The essential components of a placebo are that it has no actual working ingredient and does not actually do anything. It is the idea that it might do something that is the substance of a placebo, and it is this idea alone that creates placebo magic. If there were an active ingredient or aspect to a placebo, it would render the placebo useless in double-blind studies that compare the placebo to something that could actually do something.

Most placebos, however, do have effect because they are 'contaminated' by the very act of taking something, or getting treatment. The very action of taking something—doing something about feeling ill, provides an immediate boost in hopefulness, confidence, or energy. The act of doing something is an intervention, though the benefit has nothing to do with the placebo itself, as the placebo is inert. Even better is when someone in a 'healing' capacity (and/or a white coat) administers the placebo, as this adds imagery ranging from dead-serious authority, to Florence Nightingale saintliness, to memories of mommy and daddy kissing owies: all potent healing pixie dust. What the placebo does not do, however, is cure any actual underlying disease. If it did, it would be useless as a placebo.

Yet, if a particular placebo is impressive enough (think: ritual incantation done in full headdress), even if it was only one of many things tried (say, placebo plus massage plus exercise plus surgery plus substances with actual active ingredients)—or if the problem just goes away on its own, as most maladies do—people will likely attribute the improvement to the incantation & dance ritual. Because it did the most for the imagination. The imagination being an active ingredient in the feeling of well-being.

P: Plain, darkling   Ah, love, let us be true To one another! For the world, which seems to lie before us like a land of dreams, so various, so beautiful, so new;
Hath really neither joy, nor love, nor light, Nor certitude, nor peace, nor help for pain;
And we are here as on a darkling plain; Swept with confused alarms of struggle and flight;
Where ignorant armies clash by night. —from "Dover Beach" by Matthew Arnold; 1851

P: Priming   Psychological experiments to test the effect of 'priming' usually begin with the subtle presentation of a suggestive prompt, to see if it will bias the subject's responses. For instance, the subject of the experiment may first be given a cookie, ostensibly before the experiment starts (when in fact it has already started), and then engaged in casual discussion about cookies ('What's your favorite cookie?', etc.). The subject is then presented with a list of seemingly random words, and any inordinate cookie bias is then assessed. If the word 'dough' appears, the theory is that the subject would be more likely to think of soft, pasty cookie dough eaten straight from the tube, than the proceeds from a bank heist. Researchers who are biased toward believing 'priming' is a genuine phenomenon seem to think that all they have to do is gingersnap their fingers, and people's attention & orientation will be subtly co-opted. This theory ignores the true gingerbread of high cortical structure, and seems to believe that the brain is nothing but oatmeal with raisins. Well beam me up biscotti, but theories such as these aren't worth one thin mint. The hardtack truth, whether you are macarooned on a dessert isle, or live in a fabulous toll house with some Danish butter cookie, you shouldn't give two fig newtons about this theory. As Dr. Pfeffernuss would say, don't gaufrette about it, and do not bet your fortune cookie on ideas you shouldn't touch with a ladyfinger, or you might wind up on the shortbread end of the Twix. Meringue like that takes the biscuit.

Q: **Quagmire**   Finding a way to use the letter 'q' in an A-to-Z compendium when there are few relevant options except for that godawful 'quantum'.

Q: **Quantum**   "If you think you understand quantum physics, then you do not understand quantum physics," is a well-trodden online meme that has been associated with both Nobel Laureate in physics Richard Feynman, and Nobel Laureate in physics Niels Bohr. Though if you think you know for certain where the quote originated, then you do not understand quantum physics.

Q: Quotations, Bible style

"... old things have all passed away; all things are becoming new."

"Hold all things, believe all things, have hope for all things, endure all things."

"I have shown you the new things, even hidden things, and you didn't understand them."

"I have come that all may have life, and have it more abundantly."

R: Reason, everything happens for a   [see: Dots, random]

R: Regrets   'Egrets' with an 'R' in front.

R: Rock, pet   The Idea of Things Lifetime Achievement Award goes to advertising executive Gary Dahl, who not only managed to sell a plain small rock from Rosarito Beach near Tijuana, Mexico for 39,500% of what he paid for it, he sold well over one million at that rate in 1975. The difference between any particular rock at Rosarito Beach today, and the rocks as Dahl sold them, is that he added an idea to the rock, using an adjective. Dahl didn't name them 'Rosarito Beach rocks'; instead he sold them as 'Pet Rocks' in a small box with comfortable straw bedding for the rocks, air holes so that it could 'breathe', and with instructions for care and training. Buyers would learn that the rock would respond well to the commands 'stay' and 'sit', but needed help to 'roll over'; also, that in dire situations, it could be used as an attack rock.

S: Self, the   It just seems wrong to consider the self a 'thing'. We are conscious, awash in feeling, can be rapt with wonder, can love and be loved. Few other 'things' typically have that kind of dimensionality. Still, there is more than one kind of 'self'. The one present in the moment, with feelings of depth and range, fits Damasio's definition of 'core self'. That core self is a living presence, a biological being interacting with the surrounding world. We share this kind of 'self' with lizards, birds and bonobos, who also are fully present, aware, responsive, interactive with the world.

The kind of self that is more like a 'thing', is the kind we have ideas about, something that gets strategized like a chess piece. That self has a phone number, a library card, a bank account, and a credit rating. It can take on colorations by wearing a uniform at a job, joining the Fraternal Order of the Elks, or trolling the internet using different pseudonyms. Damasio calls this the 'autobiographical self', and ideas about it can be plain ("I like ice cream.") to grand ("I am Queen of the May.") to practical ("I know how to knit.") to esoteric ("I was Joan of Arc two past lives ago."). Since the autobiographical self is actively, sometimes inventively cobbled-together, it can be conveniently changed by rewriting the resume, uploading a new Facebook cover photo, or entering the Witness Protection Program. Some aspects of autobiographical self are more static than others, such as 'my body' and 'my mom and dad', though weight gain, plastic surgery, or industrial accident can necessitate modifications, as can DNA paternity tests. Some people have multiple autobiographical selves each with an e-mail address and social network identity, and choose which to inhabit at any given time—but it is still the underlying 'core self' that is moving the fingers as they type on the keyboard, while feeling emotions ranging from LOL to outrage in response to the different threads the different identities might be surfing. No matter how many aspects or identities the autobiographical mind assumes, from bus rider to PTA member to Napoleon Bonaparte, from the 'core self' perspective, each person has only one body, and each body has only one mind (except in the case of Siamese twins who share a brain, adults who undergo surgery to split the two cerebral hemispheres, and potential advances in brain-blending technologies) but the only limit to the autobiographical self are reality checks, often in the form of feedback from other people.

Awkward moments can ensue when the core self, with its body and mind fully alert and aware, walks into a situation where there is a mismatch between the situation and the autobiographical narrative. A student who can shred a Fender Stratocaster like a colossus at gigs on weekends then walks the halls at school like a god, but is suddenly, somehow, no longer treated like a rock star by the teacher in math class. The cognitive dissonance can be ameliorated with knowing glances to fellow students who know what a Michelangelo of the Marshall amps the student truly is, but a teacher into polka might provide no such identity confirmation, only worksheets, and scores on tests that are not #1 hits.

The inverse of not being a rock star in math class is being an actual rock star neurosurgeon at a nationwide brain surgery conference, who strangely feels like a total fraud and know-nothing whose incompetence is about to be exposed to all in assembly. The 'imposter phenomenon' was identified by Pauline

Clance and Suzanne Imes in 1978, and has been estimated to affect ~70% of people at one time or another: it's when highly skilled individuals find themselves in social situations where, despite the diplomas the trophies or the Nobel Prizes back at the office, the self-narrative goes AWOL in the current situation. Dressed differently than in the lab, confused about which lecture hall to go to, a coffee stain on the shirt, and on top of that a misplaced autobiographical narrative (or, perhaps, one never concocted in the first place). It is the setting of the surgical theater and getting handed a scalpel, that kicks skills into gear, not munching on canapés in a hotel ballroom; sitting in the hospital office examining fMRI slides gets the analytical tumblers dropping, not reading the brief bio blurb in the conference program. Being great at brain surgery is not the same skill as self-promotional pizzazz. The latter requires a script, and the willingness to act it out—a well-oiled 'brilliant brain surgeon' promo piece that can be trotted out in any alien situation, such as at conference cocktail hour. The self-story of an entire life and body of knowledge doesn't always strut and fret on the stage in the theater of the mind on demand. In fact a skilled fraudster or huckster has far greater ease playing the 'role' of expert, with complete self-confidence, than an actual expert might have when needing to 'play the part' of an expert. A skilled fraudster who has cocktail hour skills down pat, when pressed by a genuine conference-goer on stereotactic craniotomy, will know the exact moment to spill mustard on the other person's suit, or, in really critical situations, knock over the punch bowl.

Knowing thyself only goes so far—to the extent that it is even possible. 'Know thyself' is a maxim received by the Oracle of

Dephi from the god Apollo, and is inscribed at the Temple of Apollo at Delphi. Another maxim inscribed right by it is: 'Surety brings ruin'. Neuroscientist Michael Gazziniga in *The Mind's Past* compares the conscious mind to a playground monitor, frantically trying to keep track of the thousands of impulses and adaptive system goings-on that make up the mind. V.S. Ramachandran points out that neurology identifies so many components to the 'self' that there may be no such unified thing. And William James in *The Principles of Psychology, Vol 1* observes that once you think you've captured something about yourself, that very attempt changes the thing entirely: "The attempt at introspective analysis. . . is in fact like seizing a spinning top to catch its motion, or trying to turn up the gas quickly enough to see the darkness."

Knowing the self seems at best a matter of shifting splinter insights—each borne of a truth, each a phantasm—which is undoubtedly why some people who want to get a better idea of who they are look to 'personality tests' like the enneagram or the Myers-Briggs. After filling out a questionnaire or grasping at spinning tops in therapy they are then able to exclaim to others, "Hey everybody—I'm a three!" Another notch on the autobiographical belt, shifting the story of the self in the current moment, the current moment being what there really is. After all, as Damasio points out, the self in the living moment is not a 'thing', it is a process.

S: Soap   No soap, radio. Punchline to a non-joke from the 1950s. [see: Egrets]

S: Squirrel!   A sudden imposition forcefully and fully

directing all attention to one particular feature in the mental menagerie. Or, an acetate overlay book page consisting entirely of the image of a squirrel or monkey.

T: **Tiger, three men make a**   'Three men make a tiger' is a Chinese aphorism suggesting that if three (or more people) believe that there is a live tiger overtly prowling around in a crowded market, that it will generally be adopted by people at large as true. No tiger need actually be shopping in the market for the fake news to be common knowledge. The phenomenon is attributed to the King of Wei from a period roughly between 200 BC and 500 BC. The King of Wei said he would not believe there was a tiger in the market if only one person reported it; if two reported it, he would develop suspicions; if three reported it, he would believe it. If three or more people consider this Chinese aphorism to be ancient wisdom, then it must be ancient wisdom.

T: **Toast**   If you see the Buddha in a piece of toast, eat him. After smothering him with marmalade. And poking his jelly belly.

T: **Twain, Mark, quote from**   "There is no such thing as a new idea. It is impossible. We simply take a lot of old ideas and put them into a sort of mental kaleidoscope. We give them a turn and they make new and curious combinations. We keep on turning and making new combinations indefinitely; but they are the same old pieces of colored glass that have been in use through all the ages." – Mark Twain

U: **Unused Letter**   Except in the first word of the pair, where it appears twice.

V: Verisimilitude   Bearing resemblance to something true. A worthy ideal, though not always attainable.

W: Warm Bath   Rare is the office that has no pictures of loved ones warmly clustered. As things go, paperweights can't hold a candle, but then again, they're not designed to. The office generally does not approach warm bath territory, with so many triggers of deadlines and serious business, but some personal adornment, as with prison cells in Lower Saxony, makes even a barren cubicle more lovable. In *How The Mind Works* Steven Pinker explains that it is our very nature to shun drabness and emptiness and to be drawn to and find pleasure in scenes of vivid and colorful pattern, which explains why so few families choose to picnic in empty shopping mall parking lots on holidays.

It is the home where most have the opportunity to fill the surroundings with ripples and depths of gentle warmth, mementos of meaning, soul-defining souvenirs, and sometimes the actual people pictured in the photos at the office. When the things in the home bring comfort, joy, inspiration it is like inhabiting a sphere with its own life and vibrancy that both mirrors and confirmingly re-shapes the mind of the inhabitant. A home well-textured by resonances of feeling over time make every 'snow day' a celebration, and can make even weeks-long quarantine inexplicably endurable. When waking in a hotel room somewhere and realizing it is a hotel, on the other hand, it's easy to suddenly starkly miss, in what is by comparison hollowly sterile, the almost palpable textures of the atmospheres at home. For even the most basic life-forms, knowing a familiar womb-like niche must be a potent instinct to have—a bond that elicits feelings of familiarity that are like comfort and warmth. A place of security and nurture to which to constantly return, between forays into alien opportunity. Home is not just an amusing collection of things, it is a symbiotic material parallel to the self—one that mirrors, echoes, and re-confirms the breathing, thinking, feeling self—texturing experience but also reminding the self who it is, particularly useful in those moments when the self doesn't quite feel like itself.

When first moving into a new place it can be a bit barren. A tinge of joy and hope around the edges, but still sort of sobering, and not the least a little empty. To counter the starkness of alien walls and speed the transition from abode to a home there are, fortunately, tweaks and magical techniques—and all major religions have hocus-pocus for instant atmospherics. WikiHow's listing delineates how a Christian might have a priest sprinkle each room with holy water while reading passages from the gospels; that it is essential for Jewish households to mount parchments from the Torah at each doorway; Hindu house blessings include prayers and gifts, and must be done the very morning of moving into a new dwelling; Buddhist house blessing is done by nine monks with sacred water and wax candles that melt into the water; there are Islamic prayers recommended when moving into a new home as well as a prayer designed to be said three times every time entering the door in the future. All before unpacking the Hummel figurines. However, incantations can have consequences. Father Michael Schmitz in The Catholic Spirit stresses that the blessing of a thing, like jewelry, or a house, changes the purpose of the thing: it is now consecrated to serve a higher purpose. Something blessed becomes set apart from ordinary life, and being blessed or holy means living life in a different way.

If that sounds like too radical a tweak for say, your toothbrush, psychologist and spiritual teacher Timothy Hass in *The Wonder-Full World of the Home* recommends actively surveying the rooms in a house and the things in the rooms for the unique feel they each have. He suggests techniques for tuning into spaces and objects, then applying mental energy to shape them in harmonious ways. For instance, a single room can be compartmentalized in the mind into two separate spaces, each with their own feel, if that brings clarity and definition to the room. Hass suggests ways to bring calm or enhance vitality in a space by using the 'inner home' to shape the outer home—as the two are very intertwined.

In addition to the warm bath of 'things' that can be experienced in the home, in nature, or even (for those with advanced tweaking skills) at the DMV, there is another warm bath, that is just as enveloping, that you take with you wherever you go: the colorful interior decoration of the inside of our heads—the wallpapers, furniture, knick-knacks and swinging chandeliers of ideas. Though some freight trains of thought might be elaborate gothic noodlings down rabbit holes that are utterly inconsequential, and others sugary thought snacks concocted for sheer deliciousness, yet others carrots to dangle in front of ourselves to spur on the lumbering donkey-cart of motivation; whether inspired from such touchstones as books, hobbies, mass media, poetry, school coursework, museums, bustling communities, the great outdoors, art galleries—or simply a grand wallow in whatever idle daydream sets off the endless reflective capacity of the imagination, ideas are the bubbles in our bath.

W: Whitman's Sampler   For over 175 years, the Whitman's Sampler has been the iconic box of chocolates. The first Whitman's Sampler was assembled at the Whitman factory at 12th & Market in Philadelphia in 1912, and was the first candy product to employ cellophane in the packaging. Each of the chocolates in the box has its individual charm and style. The maxed out Giant Sampler 40 oz. box includes toffees, truffles, caramels, cashew clusters, and butter creams. The box cover design harkens back to grandma's place, a specter now mostly found at plantation tours and presidential libraries. Some of the earlier classics like raspberry jelly, toasted coconut, and orange cream are now just fond memories, and the cherry cordial is no longer wrapped in gold foil, but there is still the molasses chew, the Vermont fudge, and for those with more racy tastes, a chocolate whip.

Most who purchase the Whitman's Sampler do not do cartwheels over every selection in the assortment, but still find the variety enough to make it a worthwhile buy. The caramels remain square, the nougat-fills rectangular, and the bumpy ones all have nuts. Those both most coveted and reviled in equal measure are the round cream-fills. Even if soft-centered cherry cordials don't float your boat—if you find the casings lacking in cocoa solids, or that the fillings are generally excessively sweet, creamy, and oozy—at least they can be amusing, like a good read.

W: Wine   "The quasi-peaceable gentleman of leisure ...

consumes freely and of the best, in food, drink, narcotics, shelter, services, ornaments, apparel, weapons and accoutrements, amusements, amulets, and idols or divinities . . . the failure to consume in due quantity and quality becomes a mark of inferiority and demerit," wrote Thorstein Veblen in 1899, attempting to explain why people feel obliged to spend $100 or more on a bottle of wine that won't last two courses. Veblen never considered that expensive wine is actually more pleasurable than cheap wine—possibly because functional magnetic resonance imaging (fMRI) was not available until 1977. Since then, brain scans have shown that a wine labeled at $100 brings more genuine physiological pleasure than the very same wine labeled at $5. The idea of an expensive wine causes changes in the brain that alter the experience of the wine.

A study by Stanford & CalTech researchers compared a $5 to a $95 wine, but presented the wines to subjects with different price tags. Resting comfortably in the fMRI machine with wine-dispensing tubes in their mouths, subjects reported that all the samples tasted different from one another, although two pairs of the samples were the same wine. When told they were tasting an expensive wine (even if it the actual retail cost was $5), the brain scan showed increased activity in the medial orbitofrontal cortex, a pleasure-center brain region. The subjects then reported that the 'expensive' wines indeed tasted better than the 'cheap' wines. They weren't confabulating: the fMRI showed that they were having different physical experiences, thanks to the (incorrect) idea of the wine being expensive.

Neuroscientists Hilke Plassman and Bernd Weber, while noting that there may be limitations to the methodology, also found that subjects under fMRI experienced more pleasure for the 'higher priced' samples of wines identical to the 'cheaper' samples, with changes seen in the 'brain's valuation system' (an area that also responds to money rewards). They did note, however, that there are likely to be individual differences between people more susceptible to suggestion vs. those with more heightened direct sensory awareness.

In 99 *Bottles of Wine* wine packaging designer David Schuemann describes how bottle design features are similarly used to manipulate impressions of a wine's value. Expensive-looking labels have a whitish background, minimal clutter. A touch of gold on the label or foil capsule always helps. Even the color of the foil atop the bottle shades the idea of the wine toward rich berry, tropical, or buttery. Then there is the pretty talk on the back label: what it says, if you read it, is likely what you'll then notice when you drink the wine.

It appears that design elements, price tags, ideas, and expectations work together to effect a genuine synesthesia—changing the actual physiology underlying subjective experience.

X: X   Former spouse. Hey Trish!

Y: Y   "Because," gets a B. "Why not," gets an A. All other answers get a C.

Z: Fez   A smallish, taperingly conical, often red hat, with a tassle on top, and the 'z' at the end, where it belongs.

References

Books

Blake, William. Songs of Innocence. Self-published, 1789.

Brown, Donald E. Human Universals. McGraw-Hill, 1991.

Carle, Eric. Mister Seahorse. Philomel Books, 2011.

Damasio, Antonio. Descartes' Error: Emotion, Reason and the Human Brain. Vintage Digital, 2008.

Damasio, Antonio R. The Feeling of What Happens: Body and Emotion in the Making of Consciousness. William Heinemann, 2000.

Damasio, Antonio R. Self Comes to Mind: Constructing the Conscious Brain. Vintage Books, 2012.

Damasio, Antonio R. The Strange Order of Things: Life, Feeling, and the Making of Cultures. Vintage Books, a Division of Penguin Random House LLC, 2019.

Della Femina, Jerry, and Charles Sopkin. From Those

Wonderful Folks Who Gave You Pearl Harbor: Front-Line Dispatches from the Advertising War. Simon and Schuster, 1970.

Eagleman, David. Incognito: the Secret Lives of Brains. Pantheon Books, 2011.

Eagleman, David & Brandt, Anthony. Runaway Species: How Human Creativity Remakes the World. Canongate Books LTD, 2018.

Eliade, Mircea. The Sacred and the Profane: the Nature of Religion. Harvest, 1968.

Frith, Chris. Making up the Mind: How the Brain Creates Our Mental World. Wiley, 2013.

Gazzaniga, Michael S. The Mind's Past. Univ. of California Press, 2005.

Gibson, James J. The Ecological Approach to Visual Perception. Psychology Press, 2015.

Hass, Timothy. The Wonder-full World of the Home. Lorian Press, 2020.

Heywood, John. A Dialogue Conteinyng the Nomber in Effect of All the Prouerbes in the Englishe Tongue Compacte in a Matter Concernyng Two Maner of Mariages, Made and Set Foorth by Iohñ Heywood. Imprinted at London in Fletestrete by Thomas Berthelet Prynter to the Kynges Hyghnesse, 1546.

Horowitz, Alexandra. On Looking: Eleven Walks with Expert Eyes. Scribner, 2013.

James, William. The Principles of Psychology: Volume 1. Henry Holt. 1890.

James, William. The Varieties of Religious Experience: A Study in Human Nature. Longman Greens, 1902

James, William. The Will to Believe and Other Essays in Popular Philosophy. Longman Greens, 1897.

Koch, Christof. Feeling of Life Itself: Why Consciousness Is Widespread but Can't Be Computed. MIT Press, 2020.

Kreuzer, Gundula Katharina. Curtain, Gong, Steam: Wagnerian Technologies of Nineteenth-Century Opera. University of California Press, 2018.

Mancuso, Stefano, and Grisha Fischer. The Incredible Journey of Plants. Other Press, 2020.

Pinker, Steven. How the Mind Works. Penguin Books, 1997.

Ramachandran, V. S. The Tell-Tale Brain: a Neuroscientist's Quest for What Makes Us Human. W.W. Norton, 2012.

Sacks, Oliver. The Man Who Mistook His Wife for a Hat and Other Clinical Tales: And Other Clinical Tales. Simon & Schuster, 1998.

Shermer, Michael. The Believing Brain: from Spiritual Faiths to Political Convictions: How We Construct Beliefs and Reinforce Them as Truths. Robinson, 2012.

Salajan, Ioanna. Zen Comics. Ankh-Hermes, 1976.

Saunders, Kenneth J. Epochs in Buddhist History: the Haskell Lectures. Ams Press, 1924.

Stradling, Jan. The Wonders Inside: Bugs & Spiders. Silver Dolphin Books, 2009.

Veblen, Thorstein. The Theory of the Leisure Class: An Economic Study of the Evolution of Institutions. Macmillan. 1899.

Articles

Brewer, William F., and Marlene Schommer-Aikins. "Scientists Are Not Deficient in Mental Imagery: Galton Revised." Review of General Psychology, vol. 10, no. 2, 2006, pp. 130–146., doi:10.1037/1089-2680.10.2.130.

Bucklin, Stephanie. "Depressed People See the World More Realistically", 22 June 2017, www.vice.com/en/article/8x9j3k/depressed-people-see-the-world-more-realistically.

Chatzky, Jean. "One in Four Americans Has a Clutter Problem – And Could Be Sitting on Some Serious Cash." NBCNews.com, NBCUniversal News Group, 31 May 2017, www.nbcnews.com/business/personal-finance/one-four-americans-has-clutter-problem-could-be-sitting-some-n766681.

Cherry, Kendra. "The Placebo Effect Causes, Examples, and

Research." Verywell Mind, 13 Jan. 2020, www.verywellmind.com/what-is-the-placebo-effect-2795466.

Cohen, Howard, and Siobhan Morrissey. "Someone Ate the $120,000 Banana at Art Basel. Some Quick Thinking Saved the Day." Miamiherald, Miami Herald, 7 Dec. 2019, www.miamiherald.com/entertainment/visual-arts/art-basel/article238148809.html.

Commissariat,Tushna. "'Life, the Universe and Everything: an Interview with Paul Davies." Physics World, 25 Feb. 2019, physicsworld.com/a/life-the-universe-and-everything-an-interview-with-paul-davies/.

Constandi, Mo. "If You Can't Imagine Things, How Can You Learn?" The Guardian, Guardian News and Media, 4 June 2016, www.theguardian.com/education/2016/jun/04/aphantasia-no-visual-imagination-impact-learning.

Costandi, Moheb. "Uta and Chris Frith: A Partnership of the Mind: Spectrum: Autism Research News." Spectrum, 4 Sept. 2018, www.spectrumnews.org/news/profiles/uta-and-chris-frith-a-partnership-of-the-mind/.

Coyne, Jerry. "Paul Davies, Chemistry, and the Origin of Life." Why Evolution Is True, 14 Jan. 2013, whyevolutionistrue.wordpress.com/2013/01/14/paul-davies-chemistry-and-the-origin-of-life.

Dalla-Camina, Megan. "The Reality of Imposter Syndrome." Psychology Today, Sussex Publishers, 3 Sept. 2018, www.psychologytoday.com/us/blog/real-women/201809/the-reality-imposter-syndrome.

Doucleff, Michaeleen. "Drinking With Your Eyes: How Wine Labels Trick Us Into Buying." NPR, NPR, 11 Oct. 2013, www.npr.org/sections/thesalt/2013/10/10/231458853/drinking-with-your-eyes-how-wine-labels-trick-us-into-buying.

Dutton, Jack. "The Surprising World of Synaesthesia." The Surprising World of Synaesthesia | The Psychologist, Feb. 2015, thepsychologist.bps.org.uk/volume-28/february-2015/surprising-world-synaesthesia.

Emory, The Neuroethics Program @. "Neuroethics, the Predictive Brain, and Hallucinating Neural Networks." The Neuroethics Blog, Blogger, 5 Dec. 2017, www.theneuroethicsblog.com/2017/12/neuroethics-predictive-brain-and.html.

Galton, F. "I.–Statistics Of Mental Imagery." Mind, os-V, no. 19, 1880, pp. 301–318., doi:10.1093/mind/os-v.19.301.

Granado, Laura Carmilo, et al. "A Spiderless Arachnophobia Therapy: Comparison between Placebo and Treatment Groups and Six-Month Follow-Up Study." Neural Plasticity, vol. 2007, 2007, pp. 1–11., doi:10.1155/2007/10241.

Halperin, James. "Why Do We Collect Things – The Intelligent Collector." Heritage Auctions, www.ha.com/intelligent-collector/why-do-we-collect-things.s?article=collect.

Hiller, Eric The International Journal of Psycho-Analysis, Communications: Some Remarks On Tobacco 1922 December,

Volume 3, Part 4, The International Psycho-Analytical Press, London and Vienna.

Hornaday Fred. "The Ten Thousand Things of Taoism: A Meditation on the Many." Bambu Batu, 24 Oct. 2019, bambubatu.com/the-ten-thousand-things-of-taoism-a-meditation-on-the-many/.

Humphreys, Glyn W. "To See But Not To See: A Case Study Of Visual Agnosia." 2013, doi:10.4324/9780203765241.

Hurlburt, Russell T. "Not Everyone Conducts Inner Speech." Psychology Today, Sussex Publishers, 26 Oct. 2011, www.psychologytoday.com/us/blog/pristine-inner-experience/201110/not-everyone-conducts-inner-speech.

Knapp, Alex. "Why Your Brain Isn't A Computer." Forbes, Forbes Magazine, 11 Aug. 2012, www.forbes.com/sites/alexknapp/2012/05/04/why-your-brain-isnt-a-computer/?sh=a1bca3013e19.

Krueger, Joachim. "Do Others Know You Better Than You Know Yourself?" Psychology Today, Sussex Publishers, 28 Sept. 2012, www.psychologytoday.com/us/blog/one-among-many/201209/do-others-know-you-better-you-know-yourself.

"Le Monde – Toute L'actualité En Continu. Le Monde.fr, www.lemonde.fr

Lionetti, Francesca, et al. "Dandelions, Tulips and Orchids: Evidence for the Existence of Low-Sensitive, Medium-Sensitive and High-Sensitive Individuals." Translational Psychiatry, vol. 8, no. 1, 2018, doi:10.1038/s41398-017-0090-6.

Maddox, Lucy. "Aphantasia: What It's like to Live with No Mind's Eye." BBC Science Focus Magazine, 8 Apr. 2020, www.sciencefocus.com/the-human-body/aphantasia-life-with-no-minds-eye/.

Menzies, Victoria, et al. "Absorption." Journal of Holistic Nursing, vol. 26, no. 4, 2008, pp. 297–302., doi:10.1177/0898010107307456.

Milán, E.g., et al. "Auras in Mysticism and Synaesthesia: A Comparison." Consciousness and Cognition, vol. 21, no. 1, 2012, pp. 258–268., doi:10.1016/j.concog.2011.11.010.

Miller, Greg. "How Our Brains Make Memories." Smithsonian.com, Smithsonian Institution, 1 May 2010, www.smithsonianmag.com/science-nature/how-our-brains-make-memories-14466850/.

Nanay, Bence. "We Are All Synesthetes | Psychology Today." Psychology Today, 20 Aug. 2019, www.psychologytoday.com/us/blog/psychology-tomorrow/201908/we-are-all-synesthetes.

Niemeyer, Sina. Diese Fotografin Zeigt, Wie Häftlinge Ihre Zellen Einrichten, 15 May 2017, www.vice.com/de/article/9aez8e/diese-fotografin-zeigt-wie-haftlinge-ihre-zellen-einrichten.

Peretz, Isabelle. "Can We Lose Memory for Music? A Case of Music Agnosia in a Nonmusician." MIT Press Journals, 20 Aug. 2009, www.mitpressjournals.org/doi/abs/10.1162/jocn.1996.8.6.481.

Peters, Brandon, MD. "Discover What Blind People See or

Experience in Sleep." Verywell Health, 8 Oct. 2020, www.verywellhealth.com/do-blind-people-dream-3014820.

Pies, Ronald W. "'Alternative Facts': A Psychiatrist's Guide to Twisted Relationships to Truth." The Conversation, 11 June 2020, theconversation.com/alternative-facts-a-psychiatrists-guide-to-twisted-relationships-to-truth-72469.

Rettner, Rachael. "1 In 20 People Has Hallucinated." LiveScience, Purch, 27 May 2015, www.livescience.com/50999-hallucinations-delusions-common.html.

Robson, David. "It's Black and White: TV Influences Your Dreams." New Scientist, 17 Oct. 2008, www.newscientist.com/article/dn14959-its-black-and-white-tv-influences-your-dreams/.

Schmidt, Liane, et al. "How Context Alters Value: The Brain's Valuation and Affective Regulation System Link Price Cues to Experienced Taste Pleasantness." Nature News, Nature Publishing Group, 14 Aug. 2017, www.nature.com/articles/s41598-017-08080-0.

Schwitzgebel, Eric. "Why Did We Think We Dreamed in Black and White?" Studies in History and Philosophy of Science Part A, vol. 33, no. 4, 2002, pp. 649–660., doi:10.1016/s0039-3681(02)00033-x.

Shermer, Michael. "Patternicity: Finding Meaningful Patterns in Meaningless Noise." Scientific American, Scientific American, 1 Dec. 2008, www.scientificamerican.com/article/patternicity-finding-meaningful-patterns/.

Spector & Maurer. "Types of Synesthesia – Synesthesia." Google Sites, 2009, sites.google.com/site/kdimarziosynesthesia/types-of-synesthesia.

Taylor W. Schmitz, Eve De Rosa, and Adam K. Anderson. Opposing Influences of Affective State Valence on Visual Cortical Encoding. Journal of Neuroscience, 2009; 29 (22): 7199 DOI: 10.1523/JNEUROSCI.5387-08.2009

Terhune, Devin B., et al. "Hypnosis and Top-down Regulation of Consciousness." Neuroscience & Biobehavioral Reviews, vol. 81, 2017, pp. 59–74., doi:10.1016/j.neubiorev.2017.02.002.

Trei, Lisa, and Lisa Trei. "Price Changes Way People Experience Wine, Study Finds." Stanford University, 16 Jan. 2008, news.stanford.edu/news/2008/january16/wine-011608.html.

University of Exeter. "Aphantasia Clears the Way for a Scientific Career Path." EurekAlert!, 3 May 2020, www.eurekalert.org/pub_releases/2020-05/uoe-act043020.php.

Warner, Kimberly, et al. "Oceana Study Reveals Seafood Fraud Nationwide." Oceana: Protecting the World's Oceans, Feb. 2013, oceana.org/reports/oceana-study-reveals-seafood-fraud-nationwide.

Watson, Becca. "Faking It: What Do Museums Do with Forged Artifacts?" Oxbow Books, 12 May 2017, www.oxbowbooks.com/oxbow/blog/2017/05/11/faking-museums-forged-artifacts/.

Wells, Sarah. "Why Do Squirrels Bury Nuts? (and Other Mysteries)." Smithsonian Science Education Center, 28 Nov.

2016, ssec.si.edu/stemvisions-blog/why-do-squirrels-bury-nuts-and-other-mysteries.

Whitaker, Jan. "Restaurant-ing through History." Blog: restaurant-ingthroughhistory.com/.

Wilson, S. C., & Barber, T. X. (1982). The fantasy-prone personality: Implications for understanding imagery, hypnosis, and parapsychological phenomena. PSI Research, 1(3), 94–116.

wikiHow. "How to Bless a House." WikiHow, WikiHow, 22 Sept. 2020, www.wikihow.com/Bless-a-House.

Wolchover, Natalie. "How Do Blind People Picture Reality?" LiveScience, Purch, 4 Oct. 2012, www.livescience.com/23709-blind-people-picture-reality.html.

Woodward, Aylin. "Your Brain Fills Gaps in Your Hearing without You Realising." New Scientist, 10 Mar. 2017, www.newscientist.com/article/2124214-your-brain-fills-gaps-in-your-hearing-without-you-realising/.

www.ingramcontent.com/pod-product-compliance
Ingram Content Group UK Ltd.
Pitfield, Milton Keynes, MK11 3LW, UK
UKHW022214230426
12048UKWH00016BA/847